CARTA'S HISTORICAL ATLAS OF ISRAEL

A SURVEY OF THE PAST & REVIEW OF THE PRESENT

THE EDITORS OF CARTA
& MOSHE AUMANN

CARTA, JERUSALEM

© Carta, Jerusalem 1983
All rights reserved. No part of this
publication may be reproduced without
the prior permission of Carta.

Printed in Israel.

INTRODUCTION

The need has long been felt for a concise profile of Israel which will present facets of life in Israel against a backdrop of a historical survey. The best medium for such an introduction in a handy form is to trace Israel's past and present through maps which can express at a glance what may take pages to explain.

In CARTA'S HISTORICAL ATLAS OF ISRAEL each epoch of the past is surveyed through maps and concise texts with particular stress placed on Jerusalem whose expansion is represented at all major stages. A review of Israel at present isolates particular aspects of life in Israel today. Picturesque maps and diagrams give an impressional view of the important threads which make up the tapestry of life in a modern industrialized state constantly underpinned by historical awareness.

TABLE OF CONTENTS

ISRAEL — THE PAST

The Region 6
   Ancient Near East 7
   Deserts Surrounding Palestine 7
   Ancient Near East — Trade Routes . 8
   Near East Today 9
The First Commonwealth 10
   Exodus and Entry into Canaan . . . 10
   The Tribes (12th cent. B.C.E.) 10
   The Kingdom of David and Solomon (10th cent. B.C.E.) 11
   The Divided Monarchy (9th-8th cent. B.C.E.) 11
   Jerusalem and the Time of the First Temple (10th-6th cent. B.C.E.) 11
   Exile and Return to Zion (6th-5th cent. B.C.E.) 11
The Second Commonwealth 12
   Jerusalem in the Time of the Second Temple 12
   Reconstruction of the Second Temple 12
   The Empire of Alexander the Great (4th cent. B.C.E.). 13
   The Hasmoneans (2nd — 1st cent. B.C.E.) 13
   Herod's Kingdom (1st cent. B.C.E.) . 13
   Judea and the Kingdom of Agrippa II (1st cent. C.E.) 14
   Jerusalem at the Time of Jesus . . . 14
   Jesus in Palestine 14
   The Nabateans 15
   The Dead Sea Sect 15
   Roman and Byzantine Jerusalem . . 15
   Revolt Against the Romans (1st — 2nd cent. C.E.) 15
The Mishnaic-Talmudic Period . . . 16
   The Sanhedrin and Links with Babylon 16
   Synagogues (1st — 6th cent. C.E.) . 17
   Byzantine Palestine (4th — 6th cent.) 17

The Moslem Conquest 18
   The Moslem Conquest (7th — 8th cent.) 18
   Islam and Christianity 19
   Jewish Towns and Villages (7th — 10th cent.). 19
   Geonim (Heads of Academies) of Eretz Israel 19
The Crusader Kingdom 20
   The Crusades (11th — 13th cent.) . . 20
   The Kingdom of Jerusalem (12th cent.) 21
   The Crusader Kingdoms (12th — 13th cent.). 21
The Mameluke and Ottoman Periods 23
   Mameluke Rule (13th — 15th cent.) . 22
   Jerusalem in the Mameluke Period . 22
   The Ottoman Empire at its Greatest Extent (16th cent.). 22
   Ottoman Rule (17th cent.) 23
   Christian Foundations in Palestine (ca. 1830-1914) 23
Jewish Revival 24
   Jerusalem's Jewish Quarter and New Suburbs (19th cent.) 24
   The Old 'Yishuv' (Palestine's Jewish Population) 25
   Towns and Villages of the First and Second Aliyah 25
The British Mandate 26
   Unrest During the Mandate 27
   Illegal Immigration to Palestine . . . 27
   Jerusalem at the Time of the British Conquest, 1917 27
   The First Partition of Palestine, 1922 . 27
The United Nations Partition Plan, 1947 28
   U.N. General Assembly Vote, 29 November, 1947 28
   The Second Partition of Palestine, 1947 29
The War of Independence 30
   The Siege of Jerusalem, 1948-49 . . . 30

The Arab Invasion, 15 May 1948	31
The War of Independence and Armistice Lines	31
Aliyah (Immigration)	32
From Europe	32
From Arab Countries	33
The Sinai Campaign	35
The "Fidayun" 1954-56	34
The Sinai Campaign, 1956	34
Jerusalem Divided, 1949-67	35
The Six-Day War	36
The Jordanian Attack on Jerusalem, 1967	36
Jerusalem Reunited	36
The Six-Day War, June 1967	37
Cease-Fire Lines, 1967	37
The Yom Kippur War	38
Open Bridges Across the Jordan	38
Egyptian Attack	39
Israeli Counter-Attack	39
Syrian Attack	39
Israeli Counter-Attack	39
Disengagement and Interim Agreements	40
Egypt — Disengagement, 1974	40
Egypt — Interim Agreement, 1975	40
Syria — Disengagement, 1974	41
Peace with Egypt	42
Israel's Withdrawal from Sinai and Limited Forces Zones	43
"Peace for Galilee" Operation 1982	44
Operation "Peace for Galilee"	45

ISRAEL — TODAY

Topography	46
Geographical Regions	46
Summer Climate	47
Winter Climate	47
Rivers and Springs	48
Vegetation	48
Population	49
Government in Israel	50
Localities and Population by Municipal Status	50
Local Administration	51
Aliyah (Immigration) and Absorption	52
Immigration by Period	52
Immigrant Absorption	53
The Development Region: A New Social Concept	54
The Lachish Plan	54
Development Towns and Local Centres	55
Economic Development and Industry	56
Consumption of Electricity in Industry	56
Industry and Development	57
Labour Movements	58
General Workers' Sick Fund — Kupat Holim	58
Histadrut and Kibbutz Industries	59
Private Enterprise	60
Businesses by Type of Organization	60
Distribution of Industry by Branches	61
Communities	62
Ethnic Communities	63
Religious Life	64
Holy Places in Jerusalem	64
Holy Sites in Israel	66
The Scholar's Israel	66
University Attendance	66
Higher Education	67
Nature Reserves	68
The Hula Nature Reserve	68
National Parks and Nature Reserves	69
Youth Activities	70
Playground in Manasseh Forests	70
Youth Facilities	71
Sport and Physical Fitness	72
The Wingate Institute	72
Sports Centres and Activities	73
Holidays and Relaxation	74
The Old City of Jaffa	74
Holidays and Recreation	75
Map of Israel	76

ISRAEL-THE PAST

THE REGION

In the Biblical Era

Since ancient times, the Land of Israel has straddled a major international trade route and occupied an important strategic position between the powers to the southwest (Egypt) and those to the northeast (Babylonia, Aram-Damascus, Assyria and Persia).

Geophysically, ancient Israel formed the southwestern end of the Fertile Crescent that skirted the vast Syrian-Arabian Desert, and at whose southeastern portion was Mesopotamia, meaning "between the rivers". Mesopotamia was watered and made fruitful by those great twin streams, the Tigris and the Euphrates. To the southwest of the Fertile Crescent, a similarly vital function was (and is to this day) performed, for the people of Egypt, by the River Nile.

This, then, is the famed Cradle of Civilization — where, beginning in the fifth millennium B.C.E., the Egyptian, Sumerian, Accadian and Hittite cultures formed the backdrop for the Hebraic-Judaic civilization that was to emerge in the land of Israel in the second and first millennia B.C.E., as recorded in the Bible, and that later was to serve as the foundation both for Christianity (the Judeo-Christian civilization) and for Islam.

Down the Centuries

States and empires came and went only to vanish into oblivion. Israel too had its "day in the sun" — a thousand years of national life in the land that bears its name, terminated by the destruction of its independence, by Roman arms, in the year 70 C.E. But this did not spell the end of the Jewish nation and its ethos. After the fall of Jerusalem there followed nearly 350 years of cultural-religious autonomy, under Roman and Byzantine tutelage, until that too came to an end and darkness fell on Jewish nationhood.

Yet, with every last vestige of national independence and home-rule erased, and the majority of the Jewish people dispersed all over the world, a sense of cohesion persisted and found expression both in local communal organization (mainly along religious lines) and in the tenacious adherence — whether actual and physical or vicarious and spiritual — to its ancestral homeland, the land of Israel.

That country, where a small remnant of the Jewish people managed to eke out a precarious existence, was continuously a bone of contention and frequently a battleground between competing empires of the day. The fact that Jerusalem changed hands 14 times after it entered the stage of history as the capital of Israel nearly 3,000 years ago is eloquent testimony to turbulence in the region.

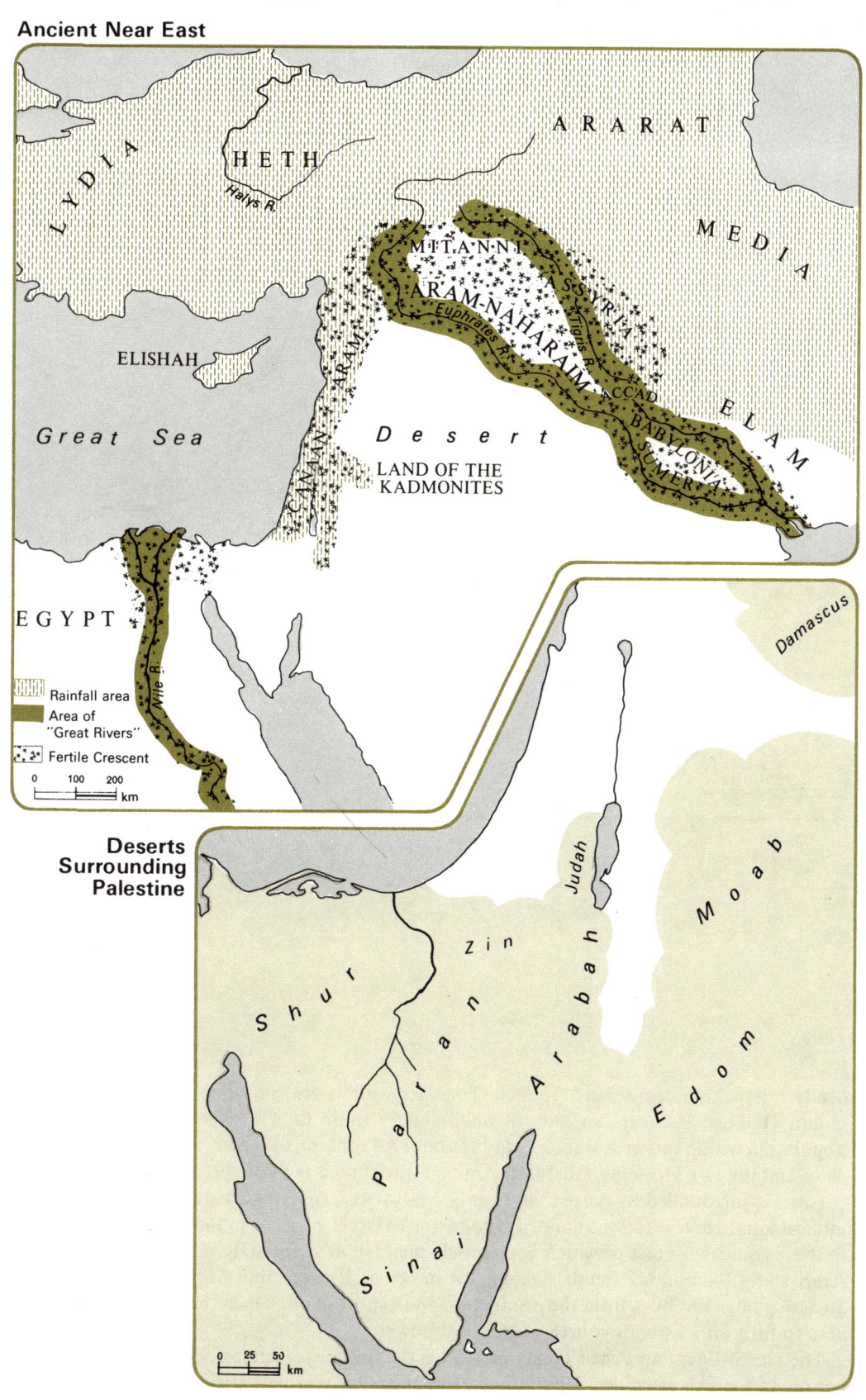

Ancient Near East — Trade Routes

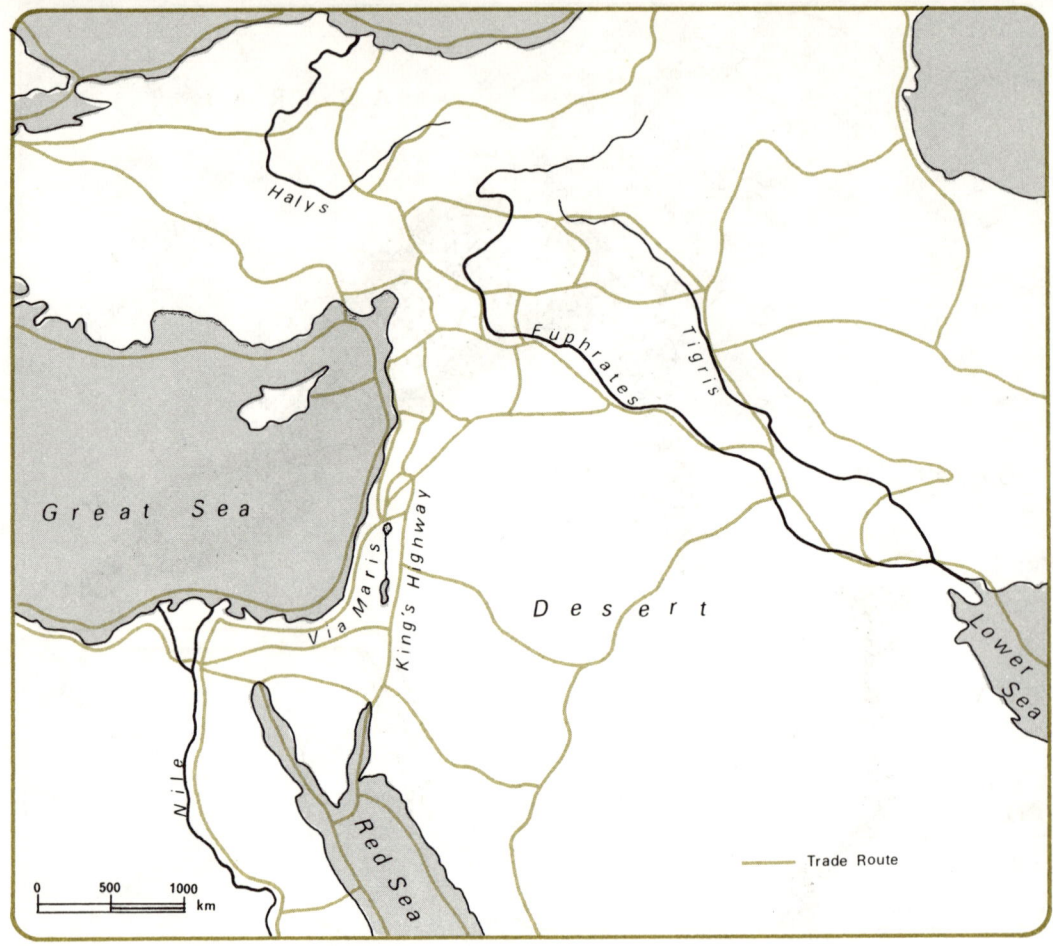

Today

Modern Israel is a democratic republic. Together with Judea, Samaria, Gaza Strip and the Golan Heights, it covers an area of only slightly more than 10,000 square miles. The population within this area stands today at about 4.8 million, of whom some 3.4 million are Jews and the rest Moslems, Christian Arabs, Druze and a few other smaller communities.

Israel is surrounded by more than twenty Arab states, covering an area of five and a half million square miles, and the majority are hostile to Israel. More than 140 million people live in these countries, most of which have proclaimed Islam as the state religion. Some of the Arab states — notably Saudi Arabia, Libya, Iraq, Kuwait and Bahrain — have been amassing huge revenues from the production and export of oil, which these states have been able to turn into a major source of political power.

The Israeli-Egyptian Peace Treaty of 1979 is the first peace agreement between an Arab nation and Israel, after two generations of intermittent war and attrition against Israel.

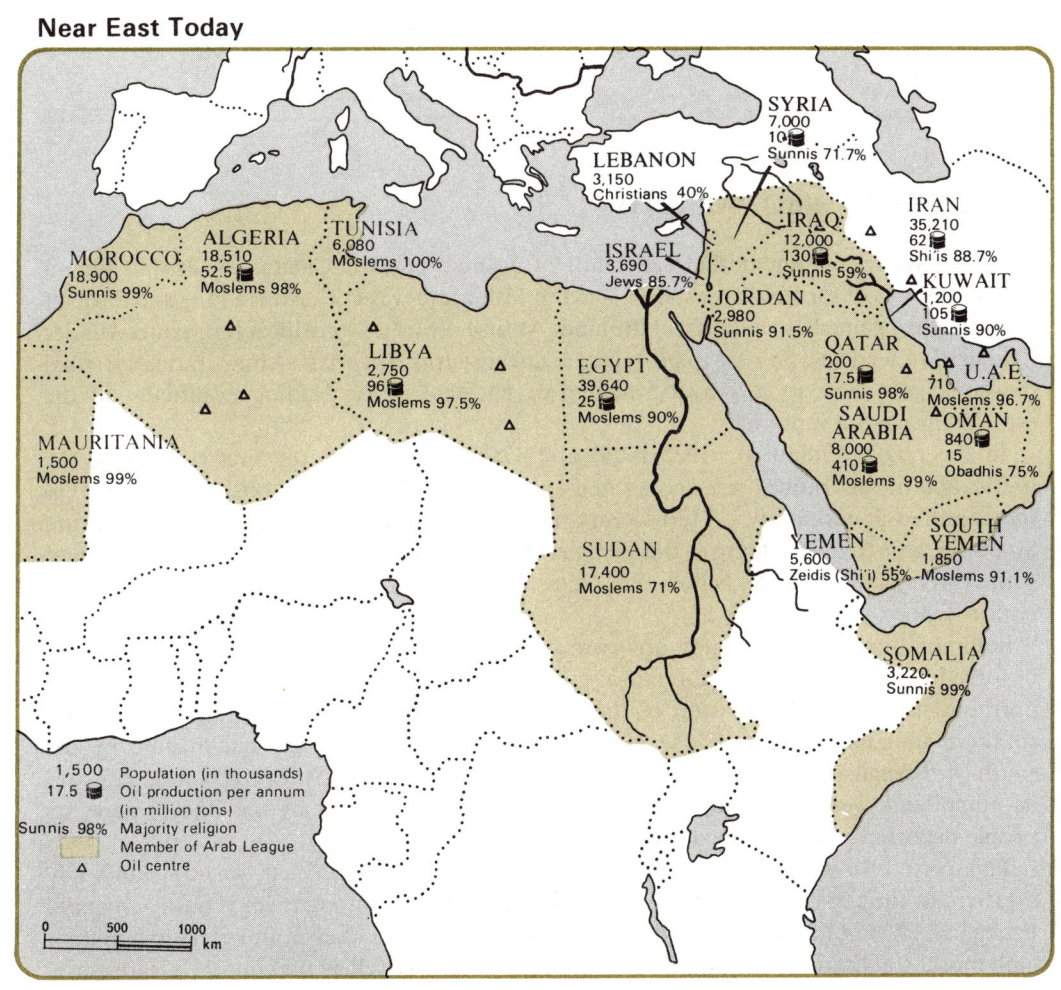

Exodus and Entry into Canaan

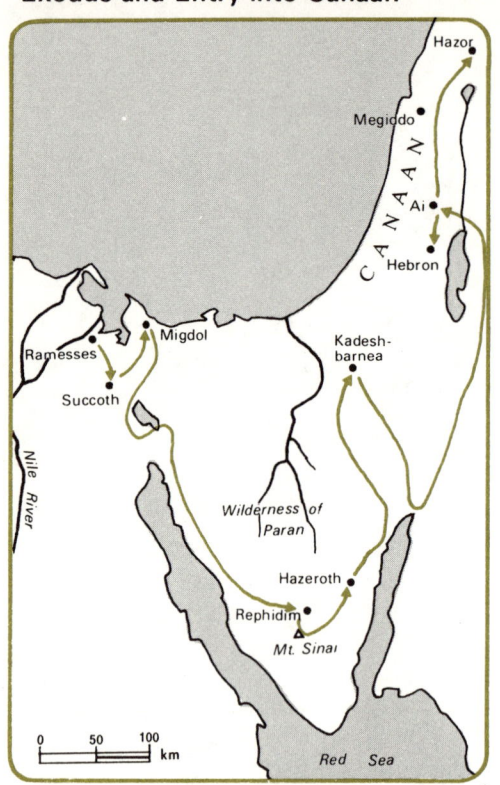

The Tribes (12th cent. B.C.E.)

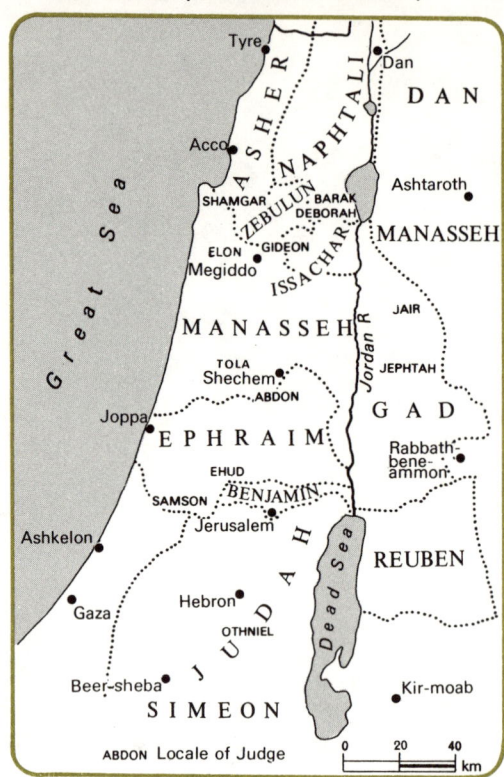

ABDON Locale of Judge

THE FIRST COMMONWEALTH

The Israelite tribes, under the leadership of Joshua, entered Canaan — at that time a scattered series of fortified city-states — in the 13th century B.C.E. After a long and difficult struggle, they gained ascendancy in the land. At first the tribes were loosely organized under "Judges" — leaders who rose to prominence during periods of crisis — but, gradually, tribal divisions gave way to a growing feeling of national unity, leading eventually to the establishment of a monarchy.

In the reigns of Saul (c. 1025-1006) and David (1006-968), the first two kings, the unification of the country was accelerated and completed. David established his capital in the captured Jebusite city of Jerusalem and bequeathed extensive territories to his son, Solomon. Due to the building of the Temple, the rapid expansion of international trade and some forty years of peace, Solomon's reign (968-928) is remembered as a high point of national glory.

Solomon's ambitious schemes, however, necessitated heavy taxation and the imposition of forced labour. His successor's refusal to ease the tax burden led to the breakaway of the northern tribes and the division of the country into a northern kingdom, Israel, and a southern kingdom, Judah. These kingdoms were now increasingly endangered by the southward expansion of powerful empires to the north. Israel fell to the Assyrians in 722, and its inhabitants were deported; and in 586 Judah was conquered by the Babylonians, its people deported and Jerusalem and its Temple destroyed.

This period, in which the nation was formed and the Bible written, was outstandingly creative. In the time of the divided kingdom, the prophets, among them Isaiah, Jeremiah, Ezekiel and Amos, fought a continuing battle to promote monotheism and to try to maintain high moral standards of behaviour among the populace as well as the country's leadership.

The Kingdom of David and Solomon (10th cent. B.C.E.)

The Divided Monarchy (9th-8th cent. B.C.E.)

Jerusalem in the Time of the First Temple (10th-6th cent. B.C.E.)

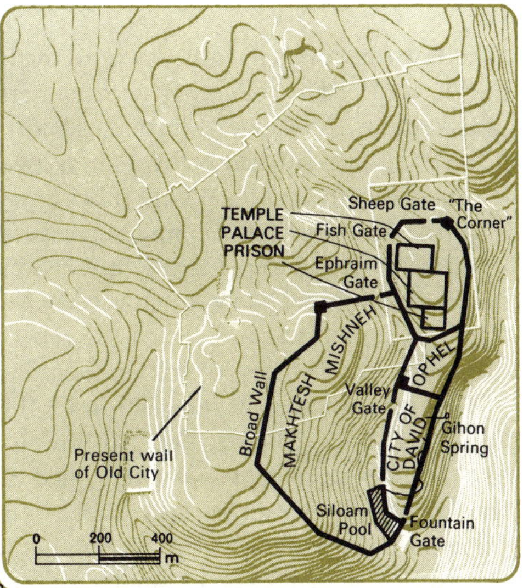

Exile and Return to Zion (6th-5th cent. B.C.E.)

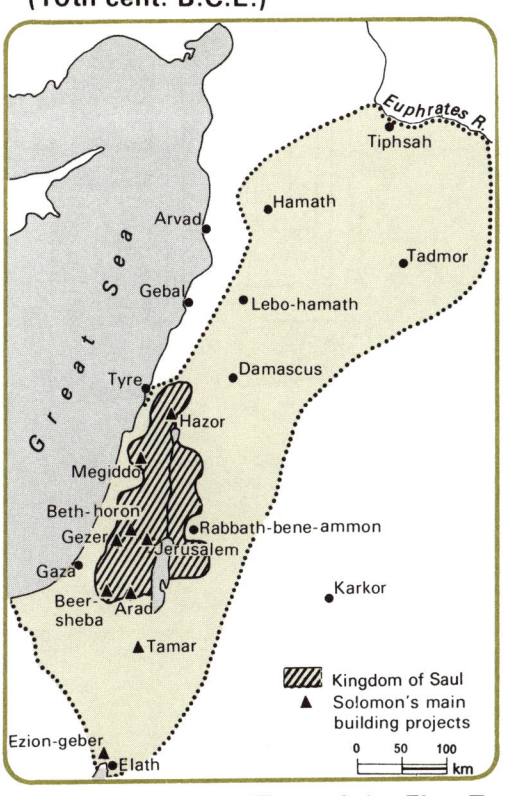

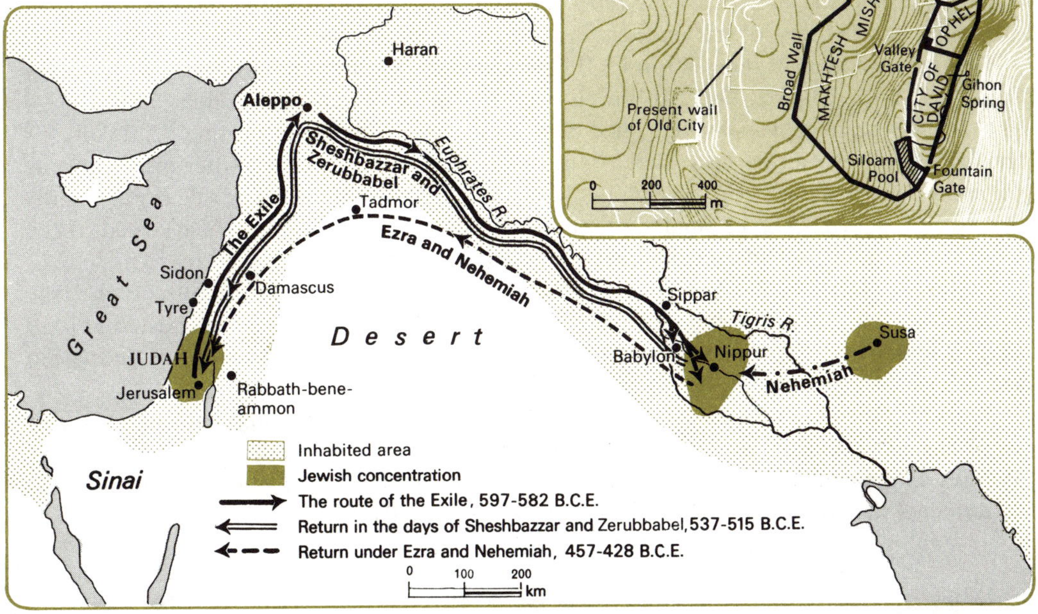

Jerusalem in the Time of the Second Temple

Reconstruction of the Second Temple

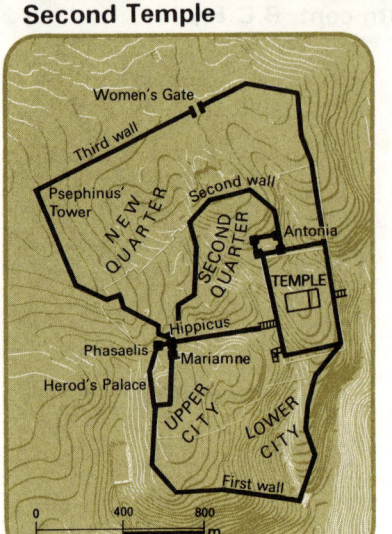
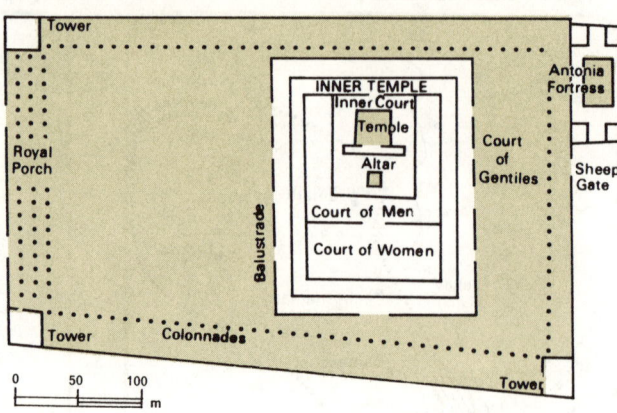

After the model of ancient Jerusalem

THE SECOND COMMONWEALTH

The Jews remained in captivity until the Babylonian Empire was conquered by the Persians in 539 B.C.E. The following year the Persians allowed the Jews to return home. Jerusalem was rebuilt, the Temple reconstructed (albeit on a more modest scale) and, under the leadership of Ezra and Nehemiah, a local theocratic regime was set up.

In the fourth century B.C.E. the country fell to Alexander the Great, subsequently passing into the hands of his warring successors. During this period the Hellenistic (late Greek) civilization began to penetrate Judah, eventually provoking a powerful reaction when one of the rulers, Antiochus IV, attempted to root out Judaism and to impose Hellenism by force. The Jews revolted, and in 164 the rebel leader Judah Maccabee liberated Jerusalem and inaugurated a century of full political independence, under the Hasmonean dynasty.

Foreign domination returned in 63 B.C.E. when the Romans incorporated the country into their huge empire. There followed a period of semi-autonomy under Herod (37-4 B.C.E.), whose reign was distinguished by its ambitious building enterprises, especially his grandiose reconstruction and embellishment of the Second Temple. After his death, the Romans tightened their grip, though the Jews managed to maintain their rule in parts of the country. Jewish resistance finally culminated in a massive rebellion which ended in the destruction of Jerusalem and the burning down of the Temple by the Romans in 70 C.E.

In the age of the Second Temple, some characteristic features of later Judaism, such as the synagogue, had already come into being. Also, large Jewish communities existed abroad (e.g., Babylon and Alexandria). Towards the end of the period, Christianity emerged within the Jewish framework.

Jesus of Nazareth, born in Bethlehem under Herod the Great, began preaching in Galilee in 27 C.E. Three years later he was executed outside Jerusalem by the Roman procurator Pontius Pilate (26-36). Jesus's ministry was one of a number of religious and political movements that flourished in the years following Herod's death.

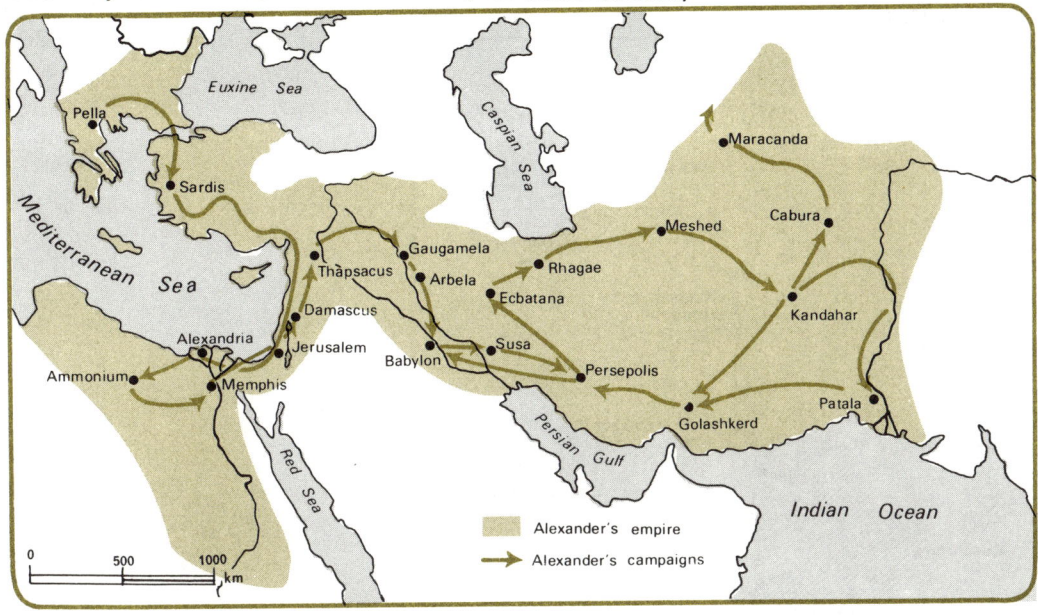

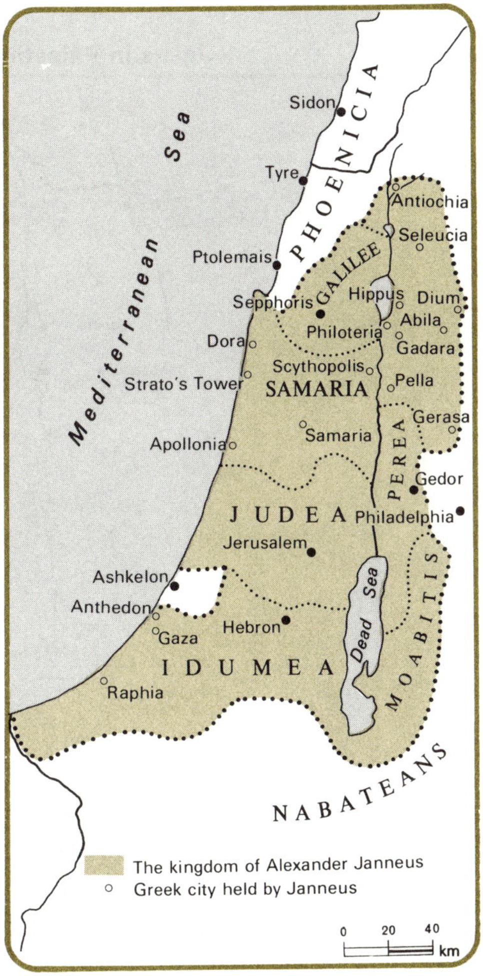

Judea and The Kingdom of Agrippa II (1st cent. C.E.)

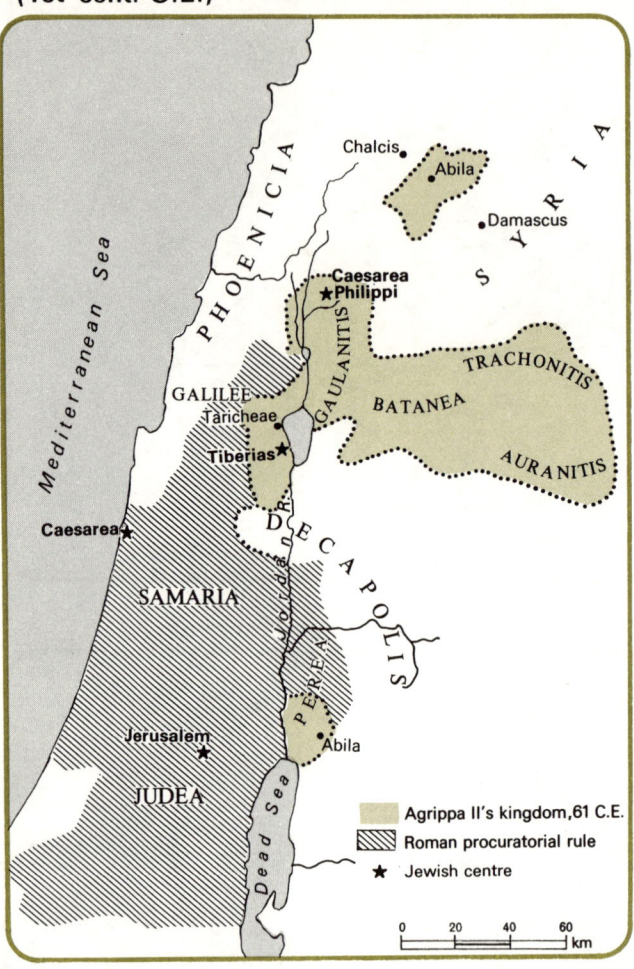

Jerusalem at the Time of Jesus

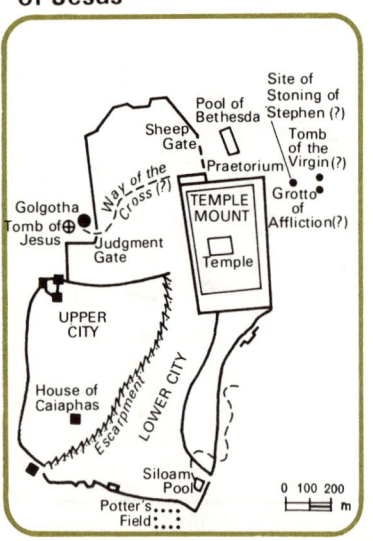

Jesus in Palestine

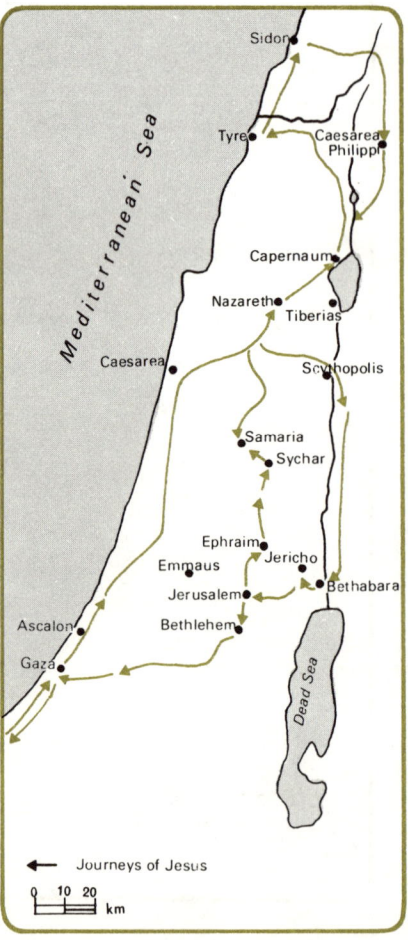

The Nabateans

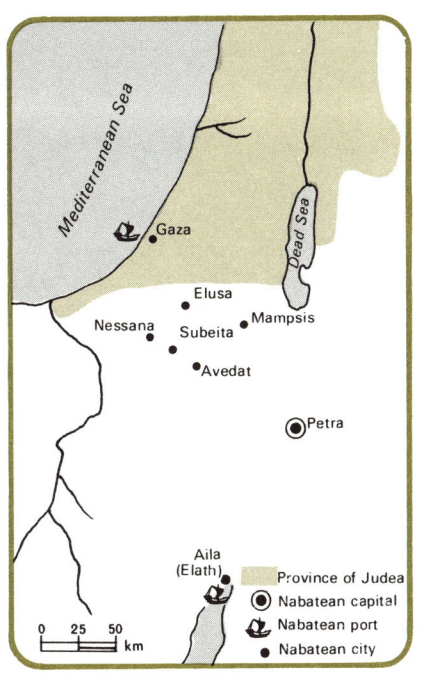

The Dead Sea Sect

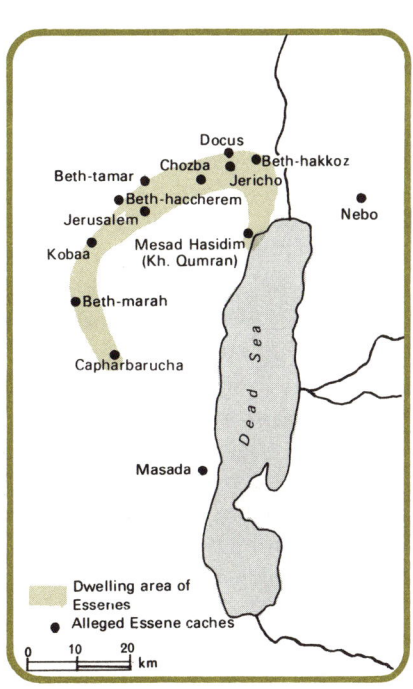

Roman and Byzantine Jerusalem

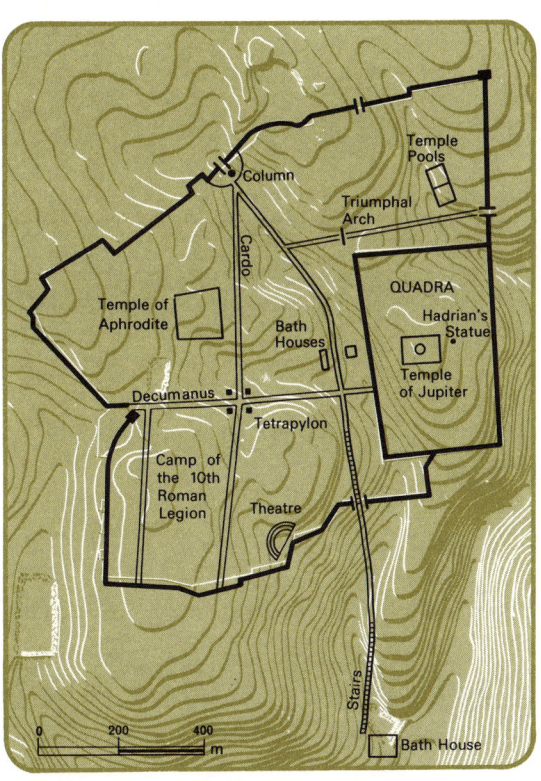

Revolt Against the Romans (1st-2nd cent. C.E.)

THE MISHNAIC-TALMUDIC PERIOD (Roman-Byzantine Era)

In 132 C.E., two generations after the fall of Jerusalem, the Jews revolted again. This last great rebellion against Rome, under the leadership of Simon Bar-Kochba, was provoked by the Hellenizing policies of Emperor Hadrian; the Jewish fighters regained most of Judea, holding on to the territory they had captured for three years. In 135, however, a massively reinforced Roman army crushed the rebels and, in a veritable bloodbath, captured their last remaining stronghold, Bethther.

Hadrian then rebuilt Jerusalem as a Roman city, renaming it "Aelia Capitolina". Jews were forbidden to set foot in the city and were also severely restricted in Judea as a whole, now renamed "Syria Palaestina" and settled with gentiles. Practice of the Jewish religion was likewise prohibited. In the wake of all this suppression, many more Jews left the country, while the main area inhabited by Jews was in the north, the Galilee, where Tiberias became a major centre of learning. The Jewish population of the Hebron area also increased.

A temporary improvement in the situation came about as a result of the annulment some years later of Hadrian's harsh decrees.

When the Roman Empire officially adopted Christianity in 313 C.E., Palestine suddenly gained prominence as a focus of Christian pilgrimage. The situation brought some prosperity, but the Jews were forced into a state of subjection that was to continue under the Byzantine emperors.

Under Byzantine rule, the country was divided into three parts: Palaestina Prima, Secunda and Tertia. Archaeological excavations show that, at that time, the deserts of the south were in many places settled and cultivated.

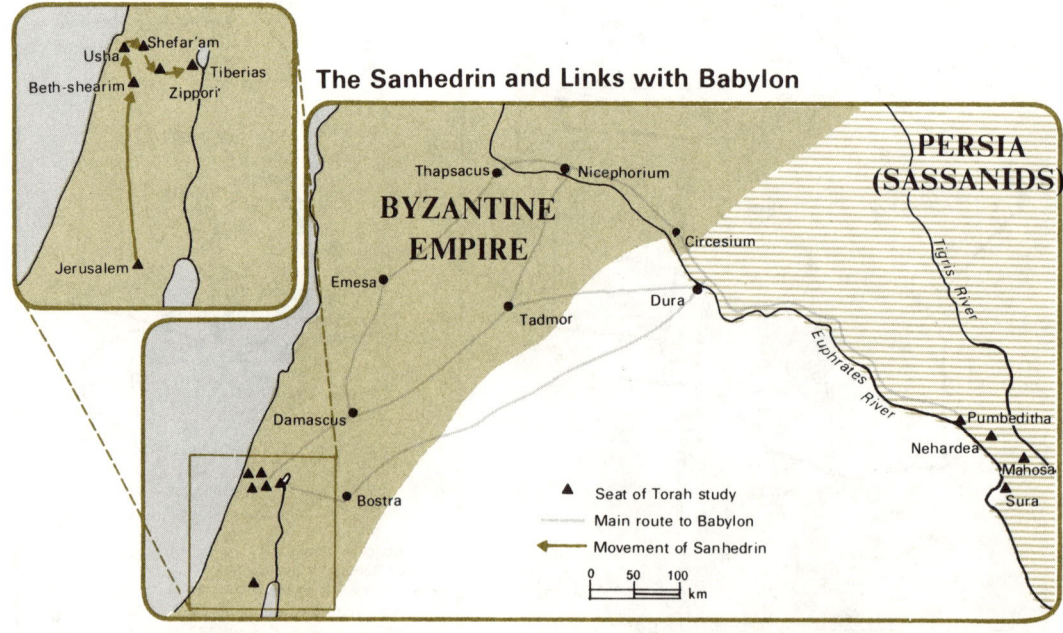

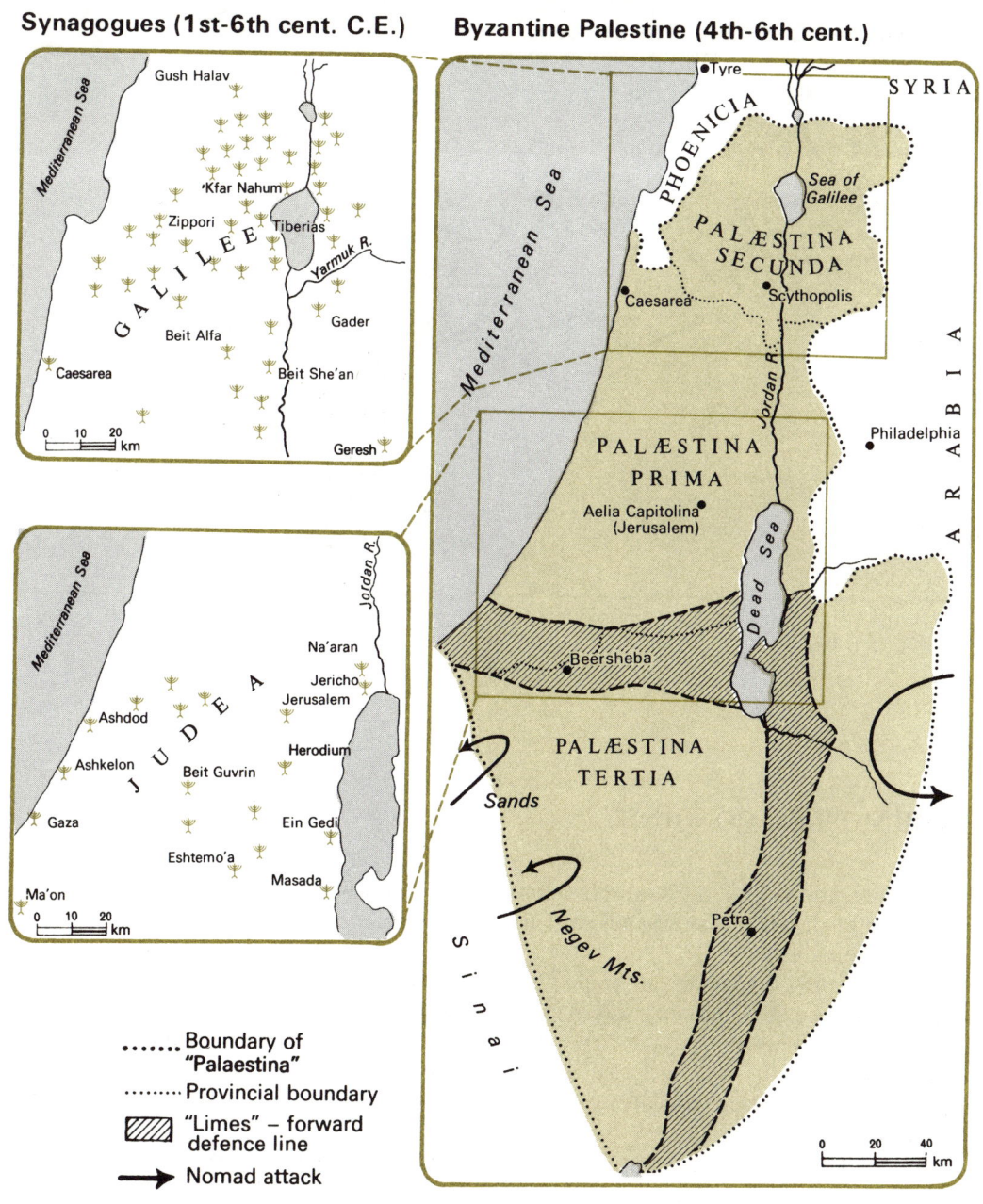

For the Jews, whose numbers had been sharply reduced by the Roman deportation in 70 C.E., the post-Temple period, up to the fifth century, was an era of consolidation and cultural regeneration. Deprived of their political independence, the Jews continued, during most of this period, to live under a self-imposed regime of Nesi'im, or Patriarchs, and to enjoy a large degree of cultural and religious autonomy in Palestine. This was the time in which the Mishnah (Oral Law) and its expansion and commentary, the Talmud, were produced. The Talmud, compiled over a time-span of several centuries, had a Babylonian edition and a Jerusalem, or Palestinian, edition (the latter actually was produced, for the most part, in Tiberias). Together, Mishnah and Talmud form one of the major building-blocks of the Jewish religion and of Jewish scholarship.

The Moslem Conquest (7th-8th cent.)

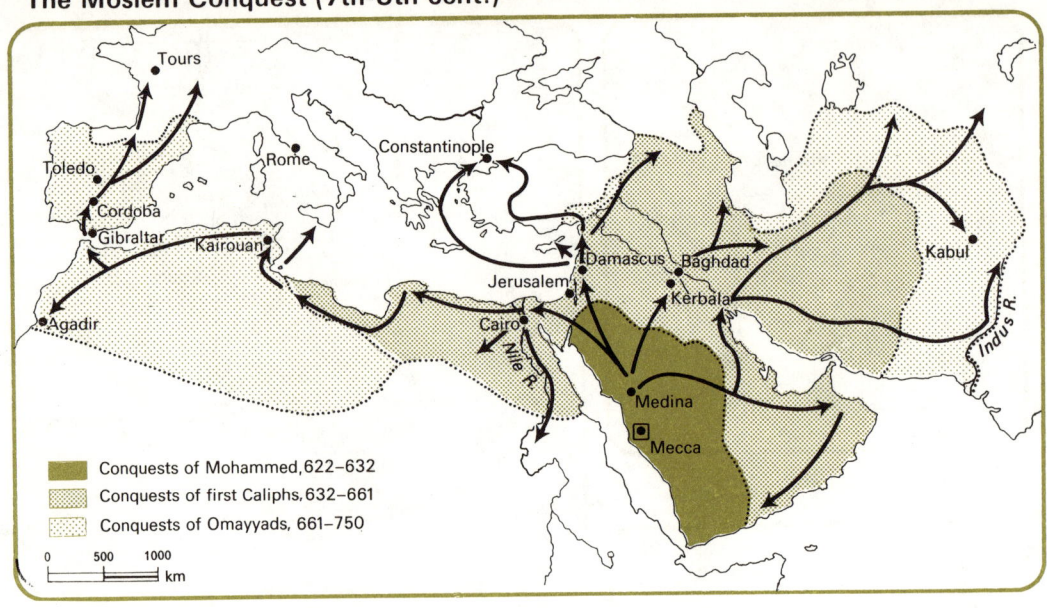

THE MOSLEM CONQUEST

In the seventh century, the Arabs, fanning out northward, eastward and westward from the Arabian Peninsula (today's Saudi Arabia), established an empire extending from Persia to the Atlantic Ocean.

Palestine was swept into this empire between 634 and 638 C.E. Under the new rulers, the central portion of the country was made into a separate province called Jund Filastin, with its capital at Ramle (the only city in the Holy Land founded by the Arabs), while the northern part of the country was included in the Jund al-Urdunn (Jordan). Although never an administrative centre, Jerusalem came to be the third Moslem holy city, after Mecca and Medina.

Internal rivalries caused several changes of dynasty in the Arab empire, the central power alternating among the Omayyad, Abbasid and Fatimid dynasties. The 11th century, during which the Fatimids came to power, was a time of increasing political and cultural disintegration, culminating in the fall of the Islamic empire to the Crusaders in 1099.

The early Islamic period saw the large-scale conversion of much of Palestine's Jewish and Christian population to the Moslem faith, and, from then until the early 20th century, the Moslems constituted the majority of the country's population. The Jews, though reduced in number, preserved their separate identity and their keenly developed national and cultural-religious consciousness.

At first, the Islamic regime was tolerant towards the Christians and Jews, but later these communities were subjected to harsh restrictions. In this period, Jews tended to abandon the villages and concentrate in the towns and cities. They were again permitted to live in Jerusalem, which replaced Tiberias as their centre of learning. In Palestine, as elsewhere, Jewish life at that time was dominated by the Geonim — leaders to whom the people looked for guidance not only in religious but also in secular affairs.

Islam and Christianity

Jewish Towns and Villages (7th–10th cent.)

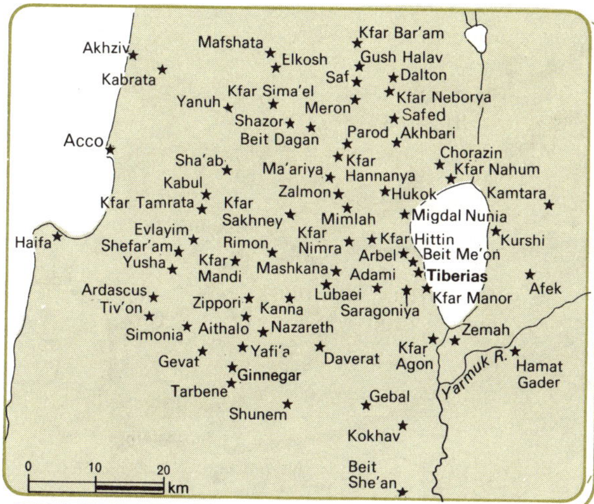

Geonim (Heads of Academies) of Eretz Israel

Zemah	862–893
Aaron b. Moses	893–910
Isaac	910–912
Meir	912–926
Aaron b. Meir	920
Abraham b. Aaron	926–933
Aaron ha-Kohen	933
Joseph ha-Kohen b. Ezron	(2 years)
Ezron (?) (b. Joseph?)	(30 years)
Samuel (ha-Kohen? b. Joseph ha-Kohen?)	988
Yose b. Samuel	
Shemaiah	
Josiah b. Aaron	1015
Solomon B. Joseph ha-Kohen	1020–1027
Solomon b. Judah	1027–1051
Daniel b. Azariah	1051–1062
Elijah b. Solomon	1062–1083
Abiathar b. Elijah	1084–1109

19

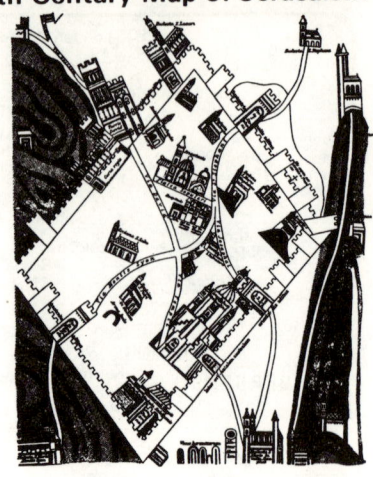
12th Century Map of Jerusalem

The Crusades (11th-13th cent.)

THE CRUSADER KINGDOM

The Crusaders came from Europe with the avowed aim of redeeming the Holy Sepulchre in Jerusalem from Moslem hands. They captured the city in 1099, slaughtering most of its Moslems and Jews. Within about ten years, they had conquered the whole country.

In the following century, the Crusaders were challenged by Moslem armies led by Saladin (Salah ad-Din). At the battle of Hattin (1187), he won back Palestine for Islam, and the Crusaders were forced to retreat. They then advanced upon Acre, which they captured and turned into a base for the reconquest of the country; but they succeeded only in regaining part of the coastal plain.

Meanwhile, where arms had failed, the excommunicated Holy Roman Emperor Frederick II managed, through negotiations, to obtain a treaty temporarily restoring much of Palestine to the Christians. Arriving in the country in 1229, he proclaimed himself King of Jerusalem. Soon afterwards, however, he left, plunging the country into chaos.

In the course of the 13th century, Crusader rule was challenged again and finally came to an end: the Mamelukes, a military caste of former slaves, rose to power in Egypt and, advancing into Palestine, drove out the Crusaders. The last Crusader stronghold, Acre, fell in 1291.

A major reason of the Crusaders' ultimate failure was their precarious position as a small and alien ruling class without local roots. Typical of their rule were the impressive castles and fortresses built at strategic locations throughout the region; vestiges of many of these fortresses may be visited today.

In this period there were Jews in Tyre, Acre, Haifa, Tiberias, Safed, and, except for a twenty-year interval following the Crusader massacre in 1099, also in Jerusalem.

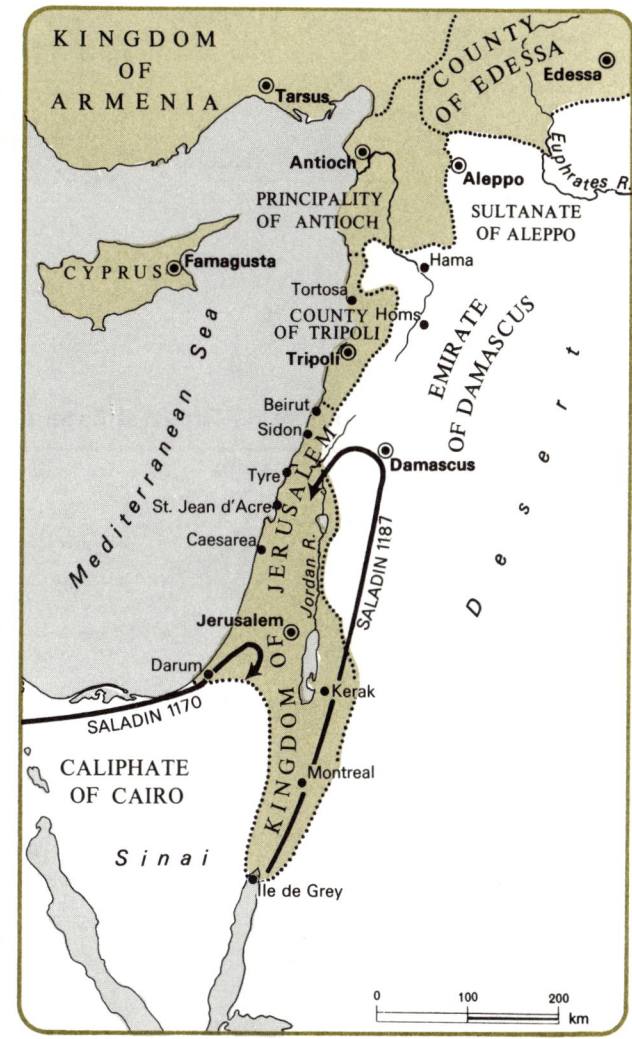

The Kingdom of Jerusalem (12th cent.)

The Crusader Kingdoms (12th-13th cent.)

Mameluke Rule (13th-15th cent.)

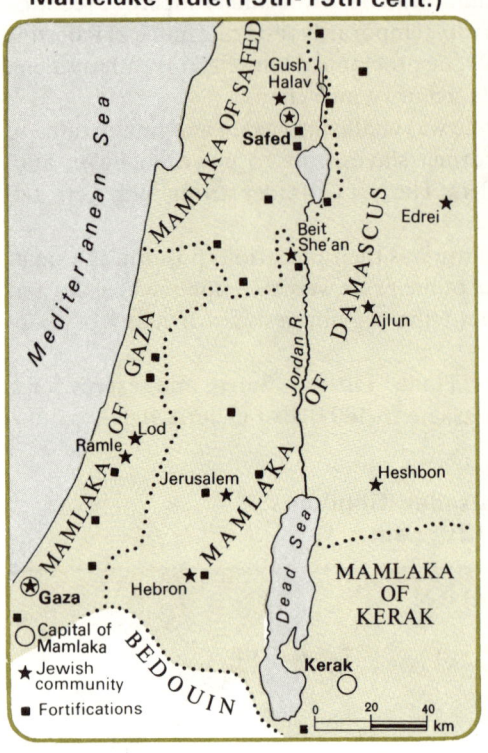

Jerusalem in the Mameluke Period

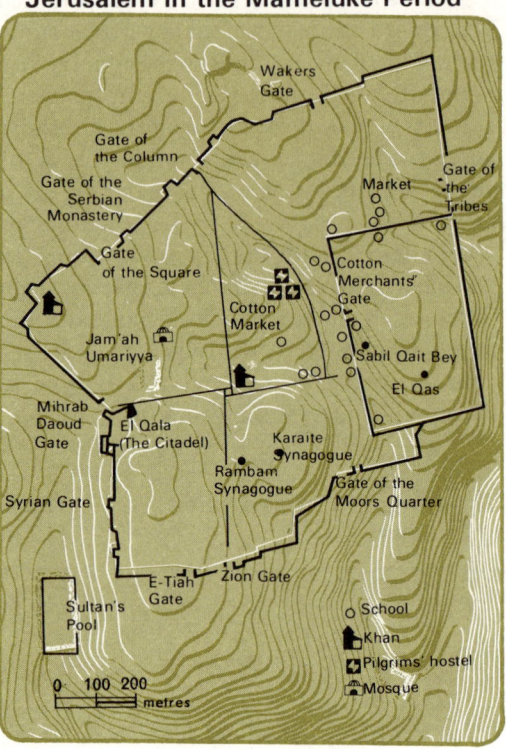

Ottoman Empire at its Greatest Extent (16th cent.)

THE MAMELUKE AND OTTOMAN PERIODS

With Mameluke rule centred in Egypt, Palestine fell into general neglect. Jerusalem had no political importance, though it was developed as a seat of Moslem learning. The Jewish communities in Mameluke Palestine were, for the most part, small and impoverished.

In 1516 Palestine was conquered by the Ottoman (Turkish) emperor Selim I. The reign of his son Suleiman the Magnificent (1520-1566) was beneficial for all the country's inhabitants, and probably marked the high point of Turkish rule in Palestine. Many of the Jews expelled from Spain in 1492 found refuge in the Turkish empire, and some of them made their way to Palestine, revitalizing the Jewish community there and putting Safed on the map as a centre of Jewish mysticism and Kabbala.

From the end of the 16th century, the prolonged decline of the Ottoman Empire set in. In Palestine, security became uncertain and the land fell prey to the depredations of the Bedouin. An improvement took place only with the growth of Western influence in the 19th century. Railways were built, easing communication both within the country and with neighbouring lands. European missionaries arrived in the country, bringing modern medical and educational services.

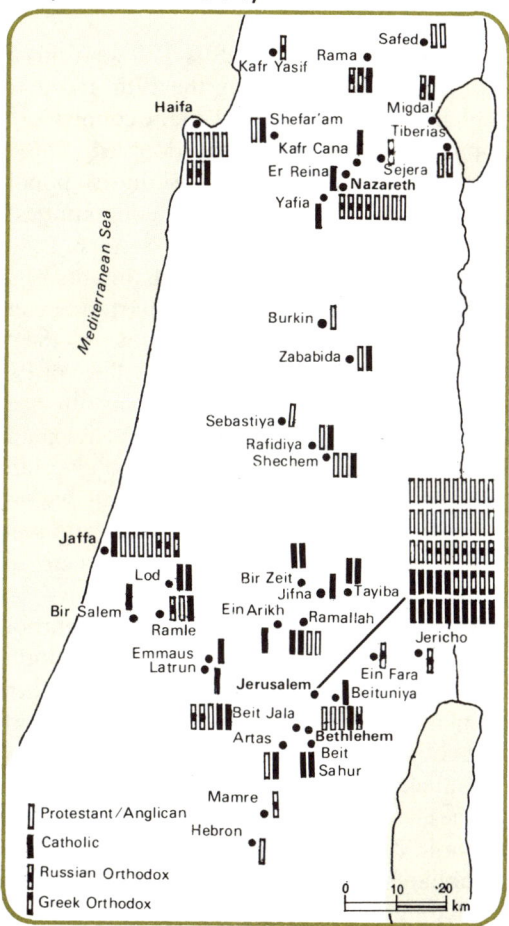

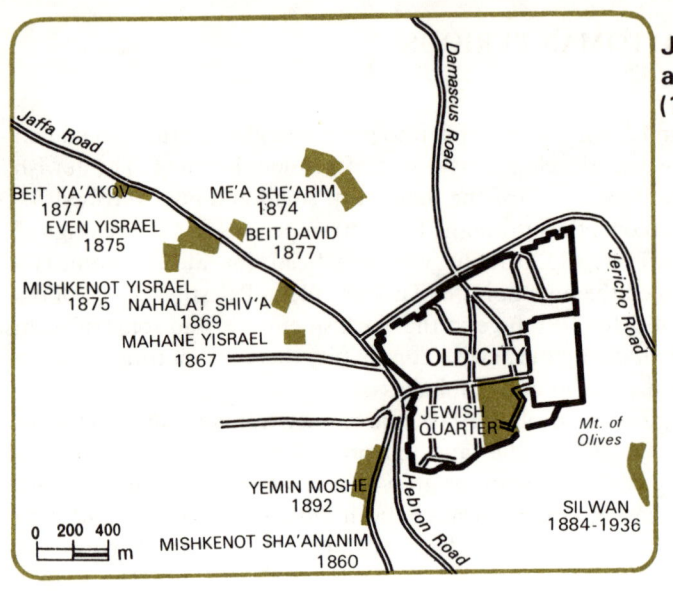

1874 Founding date of suburb

JEWISH REVIVAL

After 1700 there was an influx of Jews from eastern Europe, and towards the end of the 18th century, as well as during the 19th, more Jewish groups — both of Ashkenazi and of Sephardi origin — arrived in the country, so that by the end of the 19th century the Jewish population of Palestine had doubled. This demographic growth factor was in evidence particularly in Jerusalem, whose Jewish population mushroomed from a bare plurality (vis-à-vis the Moslem and Christian communities) in 1840 to a two-thirds majority of the city's inhabitants at the turn of the century. By 1860, Jerusalem's Jewish Quarter was fairly bursting at the seams, and its inhabitants began to leave the overcrowded quarter to build new homes and new residential quarters beyond the city walls. One group of Jerusalemites in 1878 founded what came to be known as the "mother of Jewish settlements" on the coastal plain of Palestine — the farming village of Petah Tikva (today a bustling town of 120,000).

Petah Tikva was followed by many other similar enterprises, as Jewish pioneers — many arriving from Russia and other countries in a series of immigration waves (*aliyot*) that began in 1882 — seized the opportunity to give substance to the centuries-old Zionist dream of resettling the Holy Land and reviving Jewish nationhood there.

The land, much of it inhospitable and seemingly uncultivable marshes, rocky soil and desert, was bought from Arab landowners, some of who resided in such far-away cities as Beirut and Damascus.

When World War I broke out a generation later, the face of the land had undergone a profound change. The coastal plain was dotted with Jewish farming villages, and the once bleak countryside had begun to be transformed into a gradually widening belt of green farmland. Malarial swamps were being converted into fertile fields, and in 1909 the country's first cooperative village or kibbutz, Degania, was set up on the southwestern shore of the Sea of Galilee.

The increase in the proportion of land under cultivation and the elimination of debilitating endemic diseases meant more work opportunities and better living conditions for the inhabitants. Palestine, which till World War I was a land of dwindling population, began to attract a growing stream of immigrants — Jews and Arabs.

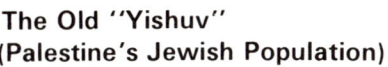

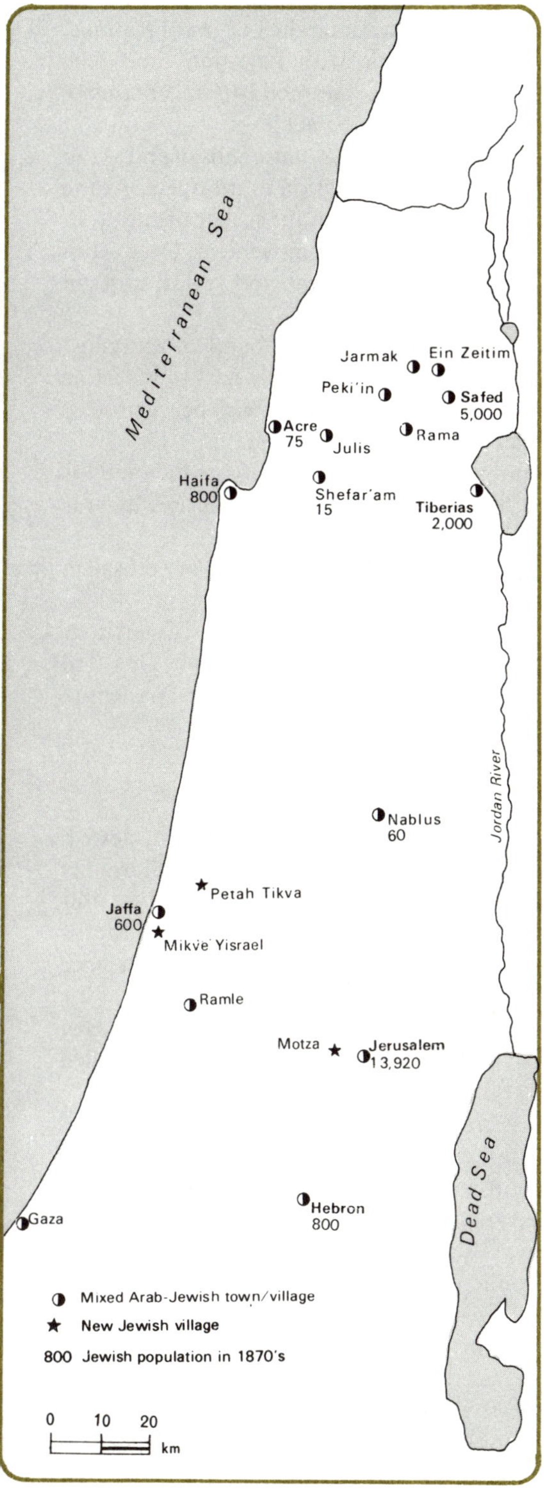

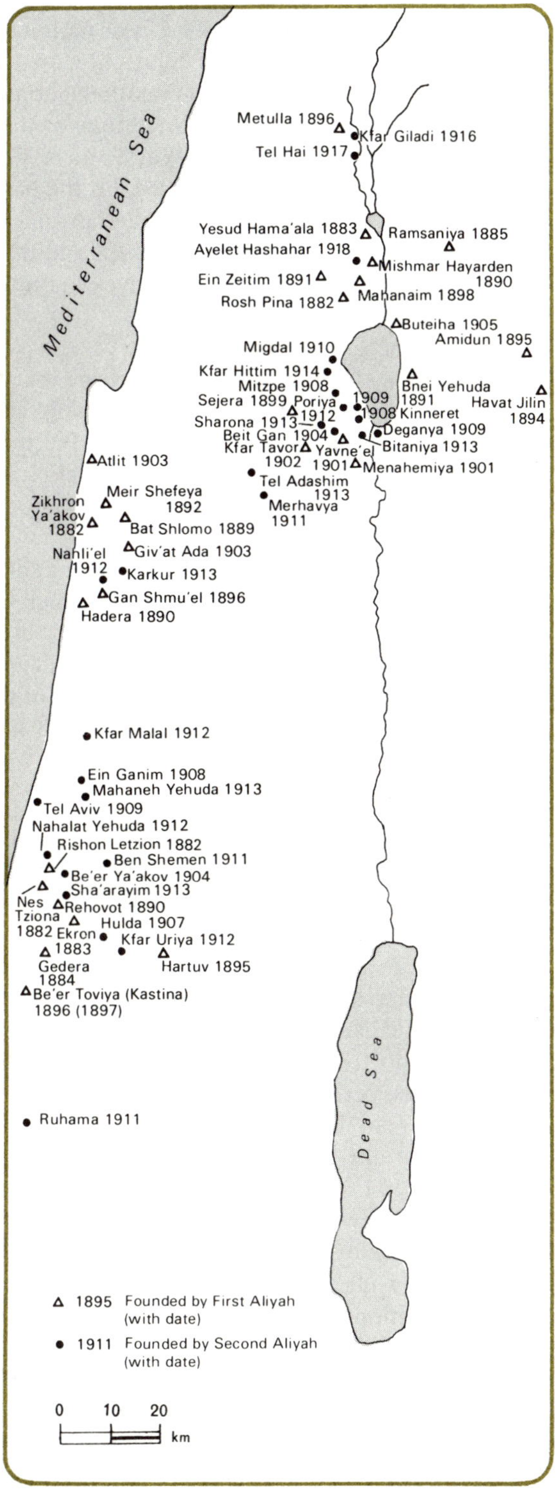

THE BRITISH MANDATE

First Partition of Palestine

After Britain had conquered Palestine from the Turks, in 1917, the British Government announced, in what came to be known as the Balfour Declaration, that it favoured the establishment in Palestine of a Jewish national home. Five years later the League of Nations, recognizing "the historical connection of the Jewish people with Palestine" and "the grounds for reconstituting their national home in that country," granted Britain a mandate to administer Palestine until such time as that objective could be achieved.

Immediately after World War I, there were signs that Jewish nationalism and Arab nationalism might come to terms, on the basis of mutual recognition and respect. At the Paris Peace Conference in 1919, an agreement was signed between the leader of the Arab national movement, the Emir Feisal, and the leader of the Zionist movement, Dr. Chaim Weizmann, confirming the objective of establishing independent Arab and Jewish states in the area.

With the emergence, however, of Haj Amin el-Husseini and his band of extremist followers in 1920, pressing the doctrine that Jewish independence in any part of Palestine must be prevented by any means including recourse to arms, the Arab-Jewish peace process launched a year earlier by Feisal and Weizmann came to an abrupt end.

The British sought to deal with the el-Husseini phenomenon by mollifying him and his followers. After arresting Haj Amin, in 1920, they later released him from prison in what was intended as a gesture of goodwill.

In the year that followed el-Husseini obtained the influential posts of Mufti of Jerusalem and Head of the Supreme Moslem Council in Palestine.

In 1922, Britain set aside the greater part of Palestine, east of the Jordan River, as territory that was to become an Arab state (as it did in 1946) and that was henceforth to be closed to Jewish settlement. Less than one-quarter of the country remained after this first partititon for the development of the projected Jewish national home.

Second Partition of Palestine

Jewish development of Palestine proceeded apace. There were more waves of Jewish immigration — first from eastern Europe and, after the rise of Hitler in 1932, from Germany as well. Many farming villages (*kibbutzim* and *moshavim*) were founded, agriculture and industry developed and national institutions established. In the wake of repeated, Mufti-initiated Arab attacks on these Jewish communities and enterprises, the Haganah (defence force) came into being; this became the nucleus of the future Israel Defence Forces.

The expansion of economic activity and opportunities in Palestine attracted thousands of immigrants from the neighbouring Arab lands, so that both Jewish and Arab ranks swelled during the period between the two world wars.

Jewish development, however, came up against growing Arab nationalism. Arab leaders fomented anti-Jewish riots, hoping, correctly, that the British would respond by limiting the admittance of Jewish immigrants. Matters came to a head after the Nazi mass-murder of European Jewry during World War II, when survivors attempting to enter Palestine were turned back by the British. Thwarted by the law, refugees then began to enter the country illegally, while, within Palestine, Jewish underground groups embarked on anti-British acts. The situation was rapidly getting out of hand.

In April 1947 the British decided to give up their mandate and turned the entire problem over to the United Nations. In November of that year the U.N. Assembly called for another partition, this time of western Palestine, and the establishment there of independent Arab and Jewish states. On 14 May 1948 the last British soldier left Palestine and the independent Jewish state of Israel was proclaimed.

Unrest During the Mandate

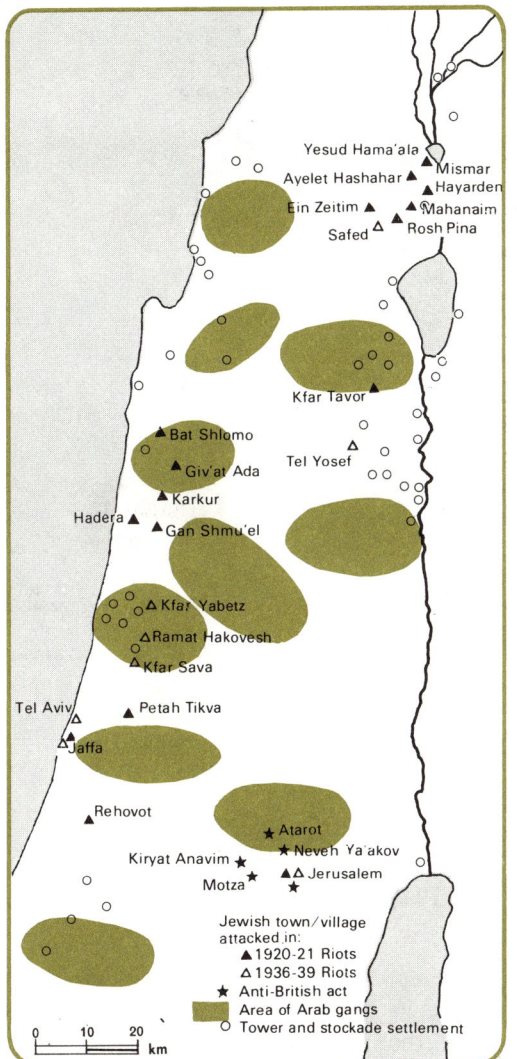

"Illegal" Immigration to Palestine

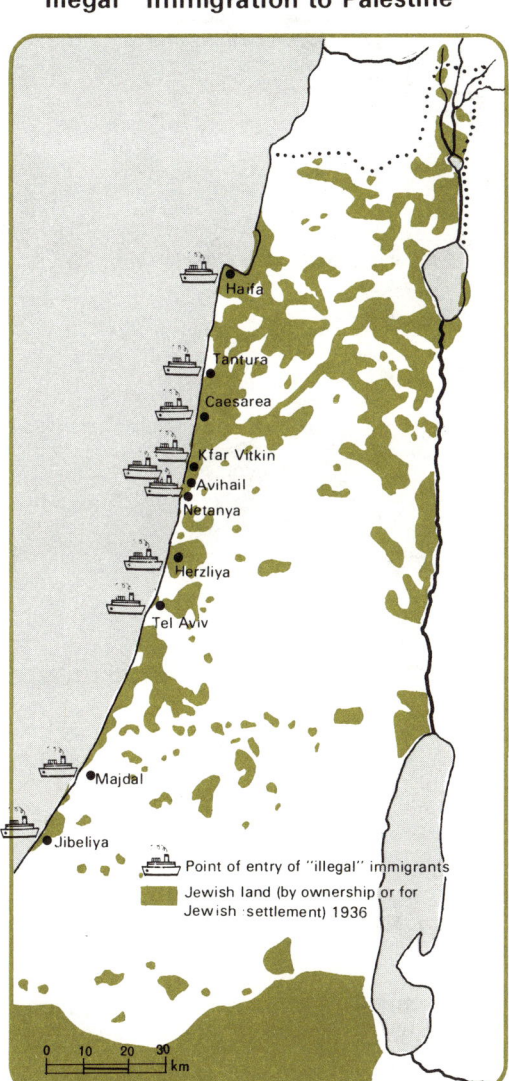

Jerusalem at the Time of the British Conquest, 1917.

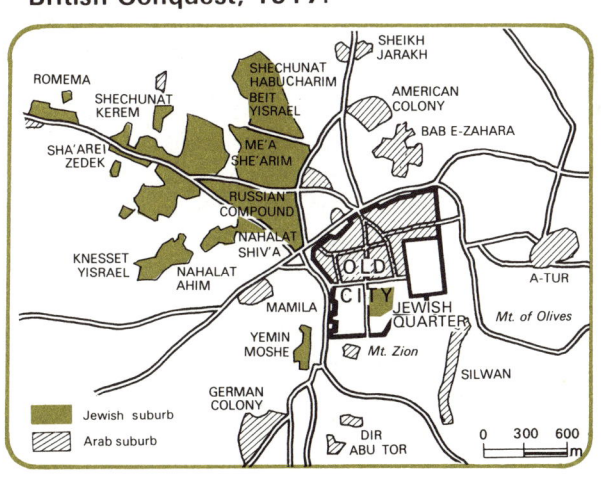

The First Partition of Palestine, 1922

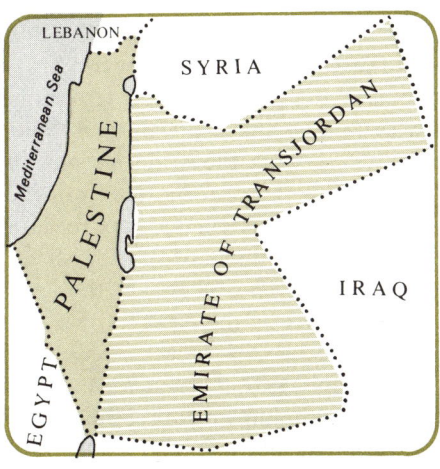

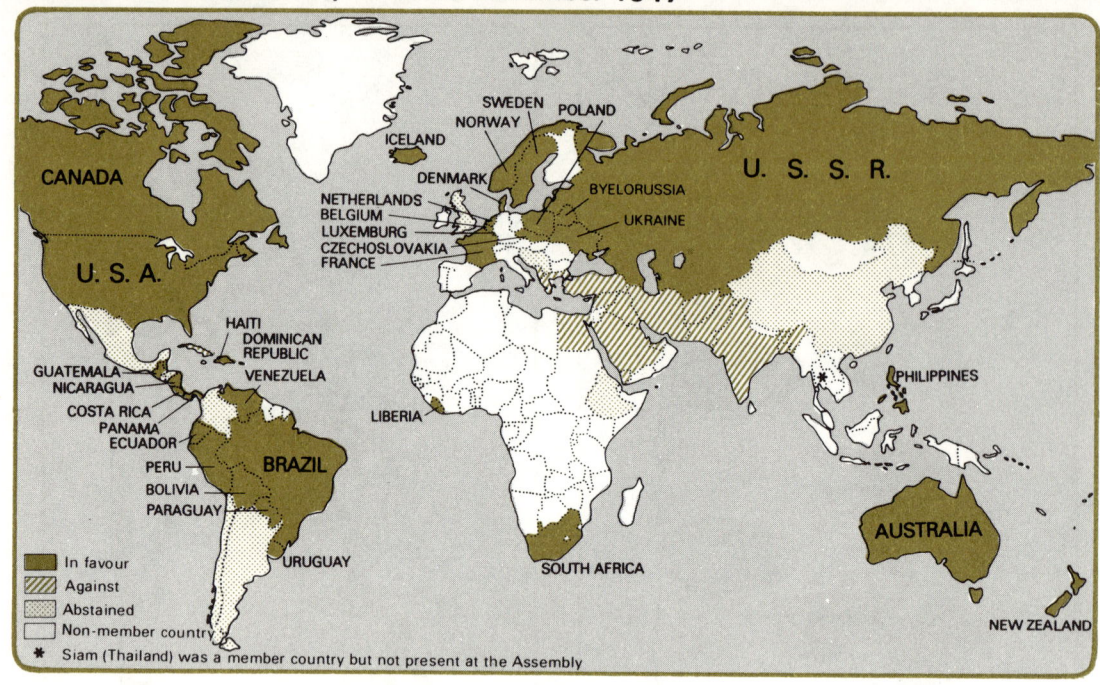

U.N. General Assembly Vote, 29 November 1947

THE UNITED NATIONS PARTITION PLAN, 1947

The U.N. Partition plan was the last in a long line of attempts to resolve the conflicting claims of Arabs and Jews. It was preceded in 1937 by the Peel Commission, in 1938 by the Woodhead Commission, which put forward two plans, the Morrison-Grady scheme and the Anglo-American Enquiry Commission in 1946. The Jewish Agency advanced its counter proposal in 1947. The question of Jerusalem was central to all plans and was the cause of much controversy.

However, none of these proposals was implemented and in the end it was the U.N. Partititon plan which was finally adopted. It divided Palestine into six parts — three Jewish and three Arab — linked at two crossing-points. Jerusalem was to be made into a separate enclave and placed under international control. The Jewish areas were the Eastern Galilee with the Beit She'an and Jezreel Valleys, the central part of the coastal strip and the whole of the Negev, while the Arabs received the rest. From the Jewish point of view, the plan offered certain advantages: it at least afforded international recognition of a Jewish state, and it granted the Jews some 55% of the land. Much of this land, however, was desert, and almost half the inhabitants of the Jewish sectors were Arabs.

This plan was accepted by the Jews, but like previous plans implying Jewish sovereignty, was rejected by the Arabs. Owing to the unexpected joint support of the U.S.A. and the U.S.S.R., the U.N. General Assembly approved it on 29 November 1947, with 33 countries voting in its favour, 13 against and 10 abstaining, including Britain. The British refused to cooperate in implementing the plan on the grounds that it had failed to win the approval of both the parties involved.

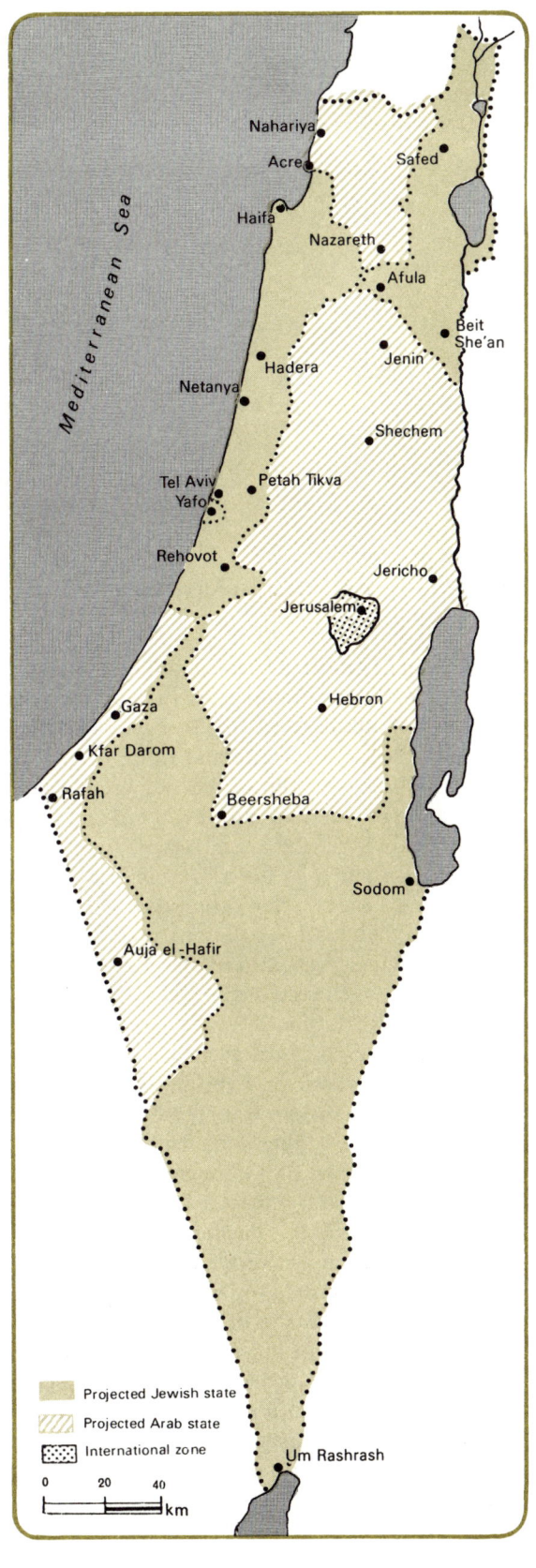

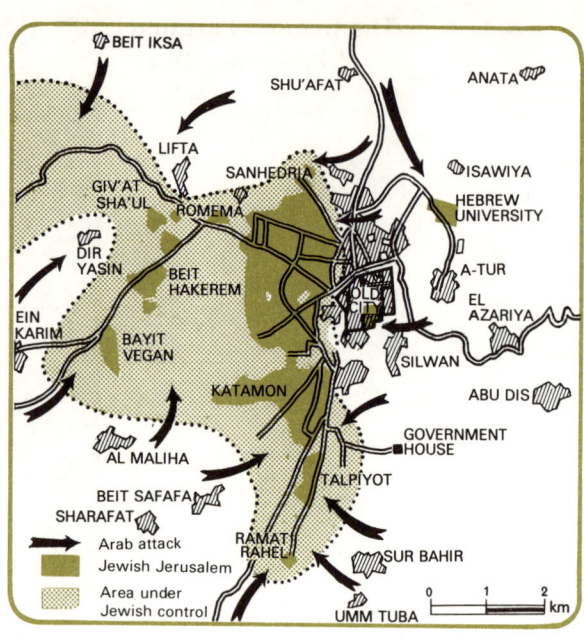

The Siege of Jerusalem, 1948-49

THE WAR OF INDEPENDENCE

Arab attacks on the Jewish community in Palestine began the day following the U.N. vote and gradually grew in intensity. In this early stage of the fighting, both sides registered local gains: the Arabs besieged and then captured the Etzion bloc of Jewish villages near Hebron, while the Jews took Haifa and Jaffa.

But full-scale hostilities did not break out until 15 May — the day after the British evacuation of Palestine came to an end and Israel proclaimed its independence. On that day the armies of Syria, Lebanon, Jordan, Egypt and Iraq invaded Israel in an attempt to throttle the Jewish state at its birth. Despite a desperate shortage of military equipment in Israeli hands, and a heavy toll of casualties (the Jewish defenders lost over 6,000 dead, or nearly one percent of their total population), the invading forces were kept at bay, though the outcome of the war was not decided till the end of the year. The Jews were generally able to hold their ground and, by the war's end, had won additional territories which had not been included in the original U.N. plan.

Under the terms of the armistice agreements signed between Israel and the neighbouring Arab countries between February and July 1949, Israel retained the whole of Galilee, the coastal plain, a corridor leading from the plain to Jerusalem, and all of the Negev except the Gaza district along the Mediterranean coast.

The western part of Jerusalem — the modern Jewish section — was under siege during most of the war and subjected to shelling from the surrounding Arab Legion and Egyptian forces. Under the U.N. plan the city was to have been internationalised, but at the outcome of the war Jerusalem was divided between Israel and Jordan with the Old City and its Jewish Quarter falling to the Jordanians.

Most (nearly 600,000) of the Arab inhabitants of the areas held by the Jews fled to the Arab-held portion of Palestine and to the neighbouring Arab states, where they could have been absorbed into the local societies and economies. Instead, they were mostly kept in refugee camps, and utilized as a political weapon against Israel. About 150,000 Arabs — Moslems and Christians — decided to heed Israel's call to remain in the country and live in peace with their Jewish neighbours — as did most of the much smaller Druze community. The Arab population of Israel has since grown into a community of some 600,000 persons, all of them Israeli citizens.

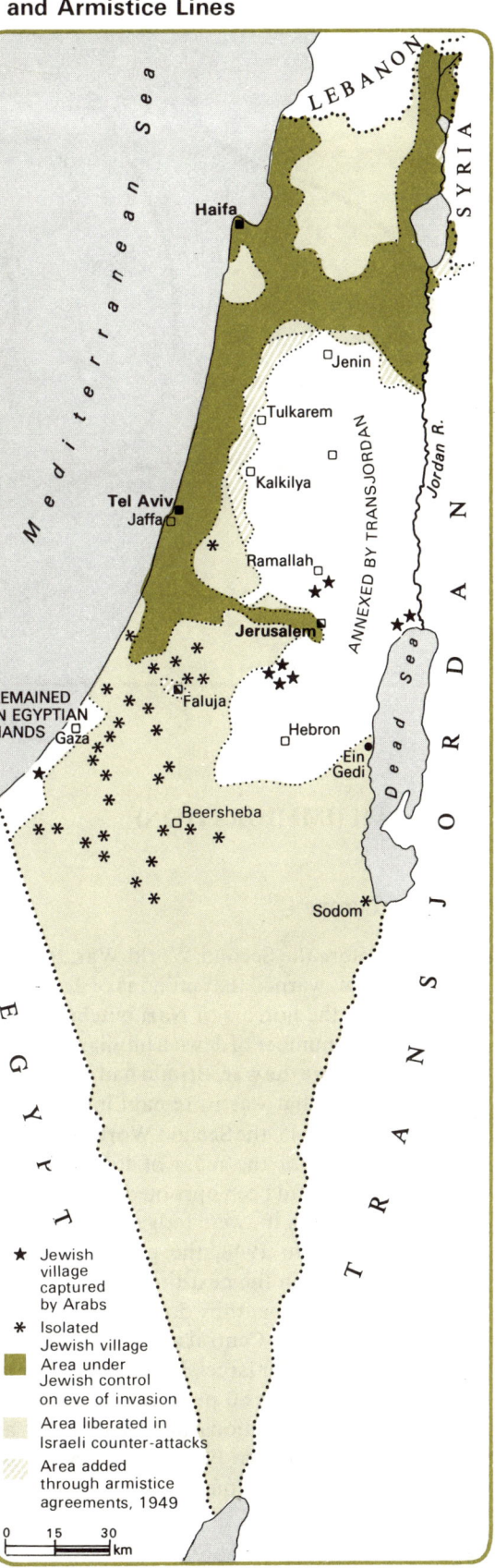

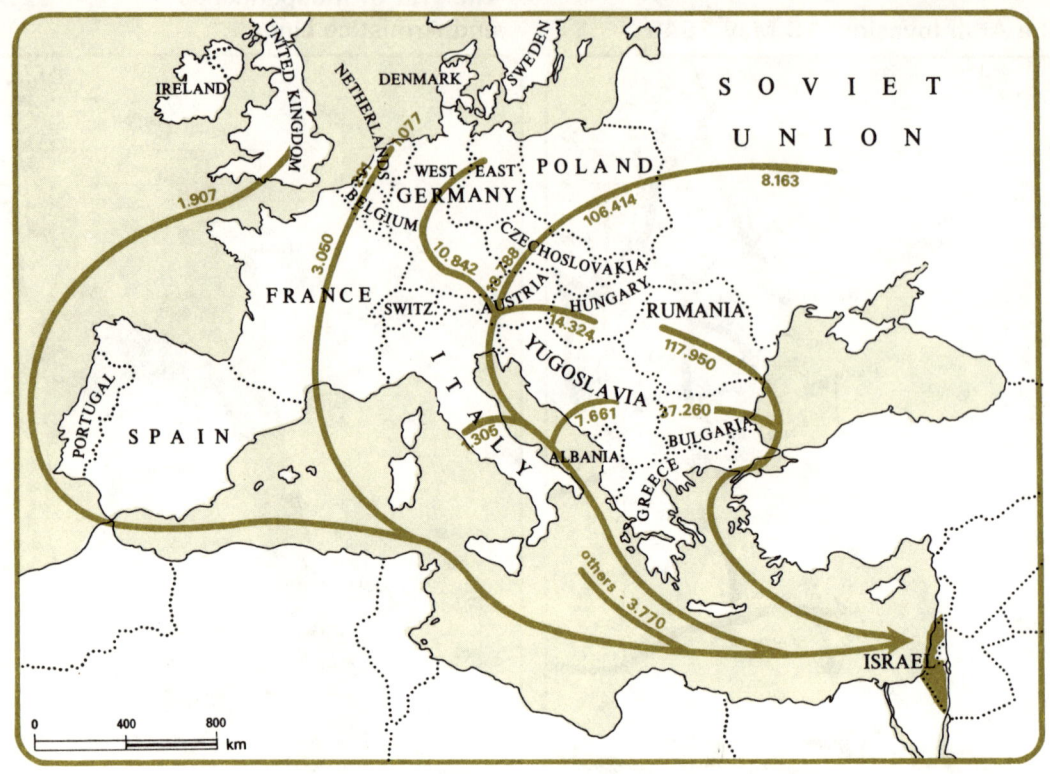

ALIYAH (IMMIGRATION)

From Europe

Years before the Second World War, the head of the World Zionist Movement, Dr. Chaim Weizmann, warned that millions of Jews would perish if they could not enter Palestine. Yet even after the horrors of Nazi butchery were known, the British government continued to restrict the number of Jewish immigrants allowed to enter the country. In the "White Paper" of 1939, before the war, Britain had imposed a limit of 2,000 Jewish immigrants per month — a restriction that was to remain in force till the British left the country in 1948.

On 8 May 1945, the Second World War in Europe came to an end. Nazi Germany had been defeated, and of the mass of European Jewry, only a handful remained. Centuries-old communities had been uprooted and wiped out. After the war most of the survivors, with no homes to return to, were lodged in D.P. (displaced persons) camps. When Israel gained its independence in 1948, the gates were flung open, and Jews arrived in unprecedented numbers. Within the next three years, nearly 700,000 people immigrated, more than half of them from Europe, thus doubling the Jewish population in the country.

Of all surviving Central and Eastern European Jews (excluding the Soviet Union), nearly half left Europe for Israel. In some cases the percentage was much higher. Of Bulgarian Jews, for example, some 80 percent immigrated to Israel. This welcome stream was eventually stemmed by restrictions imposed by the authorities in Eastern bloc countries. Hence, Aliyah from Western Europe became the main source of European immigration until the 1970's, when Russia once again permitted some emigration to Israel.

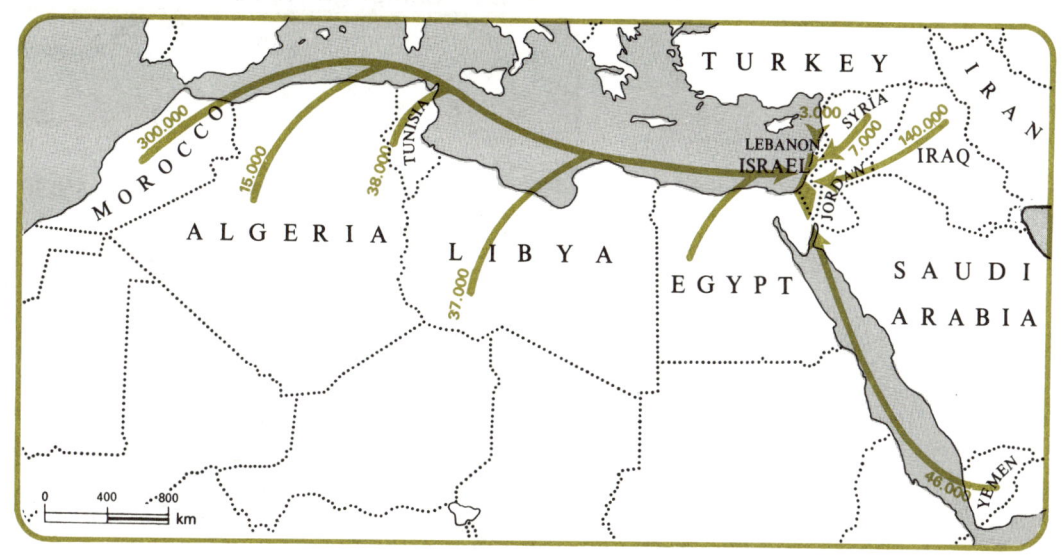

From Arab Countries

The restoration of Jewish independence in Israel had an electrifying effect on the Jewish communities in the countries of the Middle East, sparking a massive movement of Jewish families — and entire communities — from the Arab countries to the newborn Jewish state. Often this movement was given further impetus by harsh repressive measures applied by the authorities in these countries.

During British Mandatory rule in Palestine there had been a small but continuous stream of Jewish immigrants from neighbouring Arab countries. With the contemporaneous advent of the Arab nationalist movement and the war between Arabs and Jews in Palestine, Arab-Jewish relations deteriorated further, and the long-standing Arab hostility towards Jewish minority communities in their countries was reawakened, leading to widespread persecution and expulsions. With their homes and other property frequently confiscated by the authorities, many of these Jews arrived in Israel as destitute refugees.

In Yemen, the entire Jewish community of some 45,000 souls was flown to Israel in what came to be known as "Operation Eagle's Wings", completed in the autumn of 1949. During 1950-51, about 90 percent of Iraq's Jewish community — some 150,000 persons — came to Israel ("Operation Magic Carpet") — many of them penniless. So too with the Jews of Egypt, Libya, Tunisia, Algeria and Morocco.

At present, the number of Jews remaining in Arab countries is negligible, and their condition, especially in Syria, Iraq and Lebanon, is deplorable. Jordan and Saudi Arabia by law ban Jews from living there or holding their citizenship.

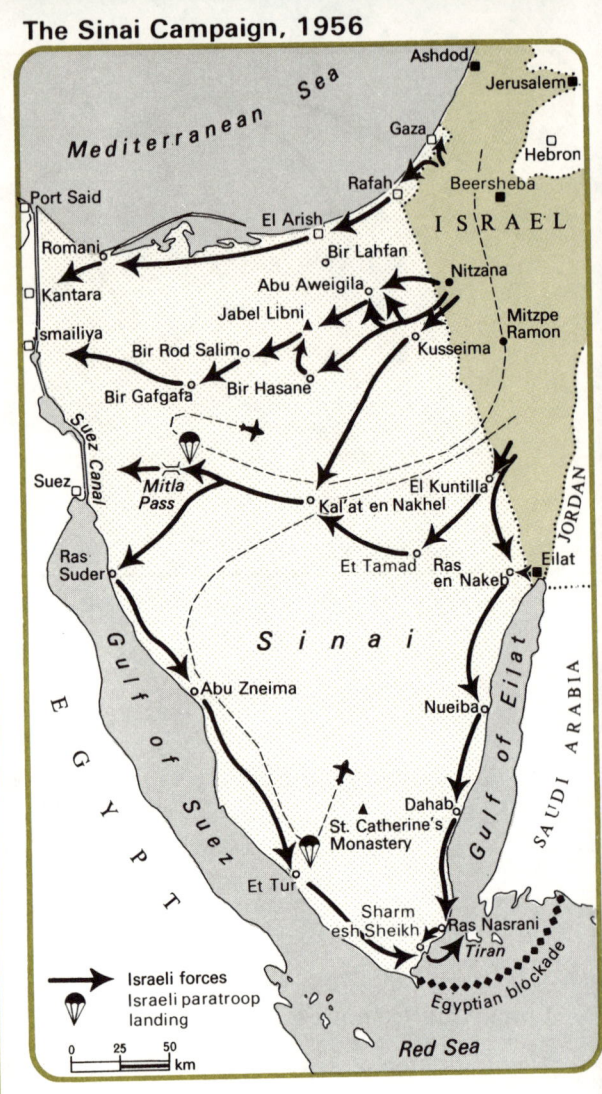
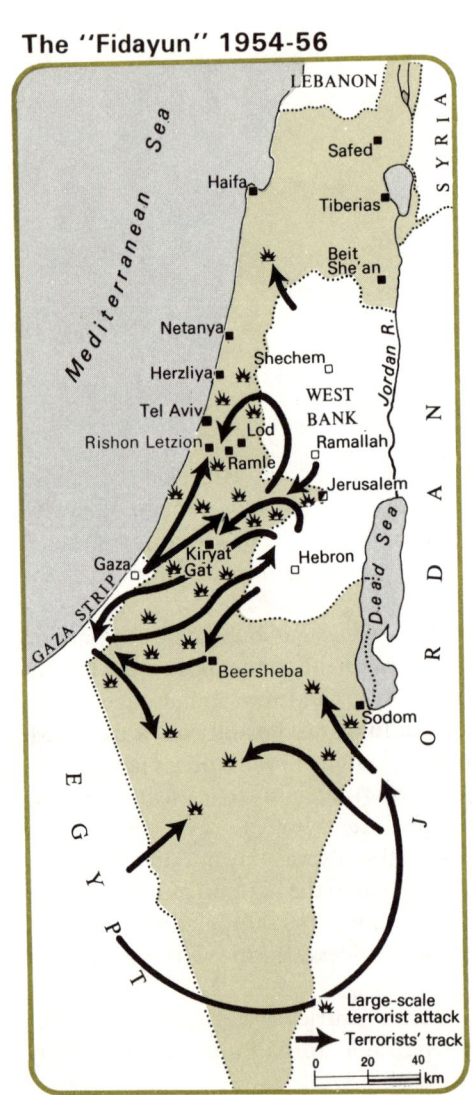

Jerusalem Divided, 1949-67

(No Man's Land is magnified)

THE SINAI CAMPAIGN

After the War of Independence, the four neighbouring Arab states — Egypt, Jordan, Lebanon and Syria — signed Armistice Agreements with Israel. The Arab states, however, continued to consider themselves as being in a state of war with Israel. Incidents along the armistice lines were frequent. "Fidayun" (armed infiltrators on suicide missions) were sent out from Egypt and Jordan into Israeli territory on murder and sabotage missions to disrupt normal life in the country. The Fidayun incursions took a steadily growing toll of Jewish lives.

Extending their war against Israel to the economic front, the Arab states organized a trade boycott, while Egypt sought to choke off Israel's maritime link with Africa and Southeast Asia by blockading the Strait of Tiran, at the mouth of the Gulf of Eilat.

Things came to a head in October 1956, when the Egyptian ruler, Gamal Abdul Nasser, newly equipped with Soviet weaponry, gathered an army in Sinai to launch an attack.

But Israel struck first and in a matter of days overcame the Egyptian forces, occupied the entire Sinai peninsula and lifted the naval blockade at the Strait of Tiran. Meanwhile, Britain and France (incensed at Nasser for having unilaterally seized the Suez Canal in July of that year) bombarded Egyptian military installations.

Very soon, however, the United States and the Soviet Union, acting together, compelled Israel and its allies to withdraw, and U.N. forces were stationed along the old Egyptian-Israeli border. It was partly on the strength of the promise that these forces would keep the peace by preventing a renewal of the Egyptian threat against Israel, and that the world's maritime nations would guarantee continued freedom of navigation through the Strait of Tiran, that Israel agreed to withdraw its forces from Sinai. (It was the breach of this promise and the summary removal of the U.N. contingents, at President Nasser's behest in May 1967, that led to the outbreak of the Six-Day War.)

The Jordanian Attack on Jerusalem, 1967

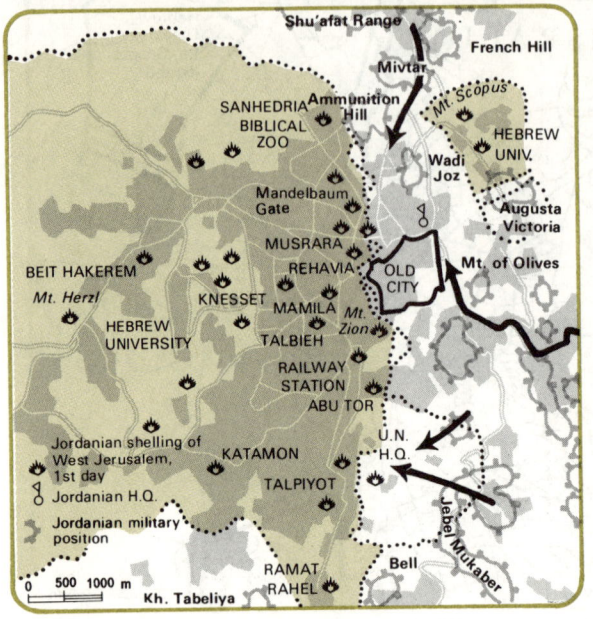

Jerusalem Reunited

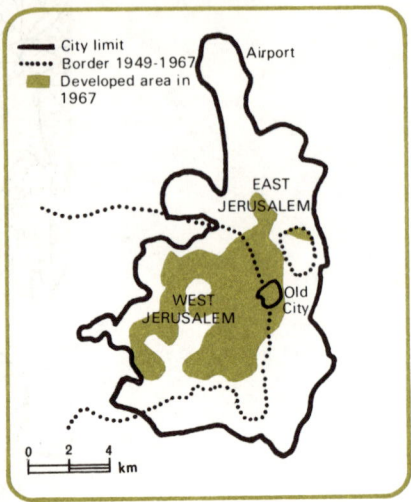

THE SIX-DAY WAR

Both Syria and Egypt had been plentifully supplied with weapons by the Soviet Union. In May 1967 Nasser, the Egyptian ruler, again amassed an army in Sinai with the avowed intention of destroying Israel. He made an alliance with King Hussein of Jordan, Israel's neighbour to the east, re-instituted the naval blockade of the Tiran Strait and dismissed the U.N. forces.

The effort to get the nations that, in 1957, had promised to uphold the freedom of navigation through the strait to redeem their pledge failed, and on 5 June 1967 war broke out.

In a lightning strike at the outset of the war, Israel demolished most of Egypt's aircraft as it stood on the ground, thus gaining mastery of the skies. Despite urgent messages sent to King Hussein on 5 June, Jordanian forces opened hostilities by occupying U.N. headquarters in no-man's land and shelling Jewish Jerusalem. In the swift campaigns which followed, Israel won, in six days, the whole of Judea and Samaria (the area also known as the West Bank), the Golan Heights, the Gaza district and the Sinai peninsula. A stirring event in the war was the taking of eastern Jerusalem. With the reunification of the divided city, the holiest places of Judaism — the Western ("Wailing") Wall and the site of the Temple — passed into Jewish hands and, for the first time in nearly two thousand years, became accessible for free and unhampered worship. Also for the first time, Israeli Moslems were able to visit and pray at their holy places — the Al-Aqsa Mosque and the Dome of the Rock.

The areas captured by the Israel Defence Forces — apart from Jerusalem (all of which was incorporated into Israel) — were placed under Israeli military administration.

For the first time since Israel became an independent state in 1948, the borders were no longer hermetically sealed. The bridges across the Jordan River opened to two-way commercial and tourist traffic. Commercial relations between Jordan and Judea and Samaria flourished. Arab workers commuted daily to Israel from the administered areas, and, for the first time, large numbers of visitors from all the Arab countries crossed the Jordan River bridges for visits and sightseeing in Israel and the Israel-administered areas. The Open Bridges policy created a new reality in the area.

The Six-Day War, June 1967

Cease-Fire Lines, 1967

Open Bridges Across the Jordan

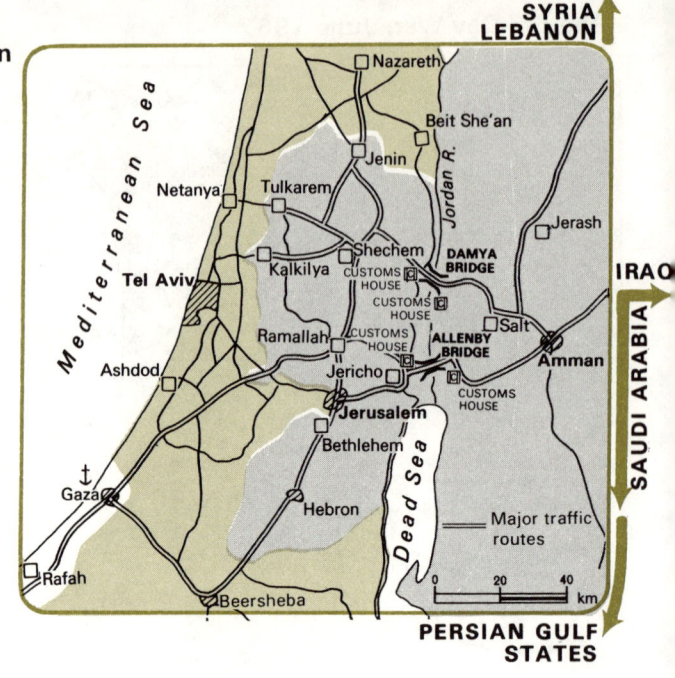

THE YOM KIPPUR WAR

Meanwhile, the Arab states prepared a fresh attack, and on the Day of Atonement (Yom Kippur), 6 October 1973, the Egyptians crossed the Suez Canal in force: simultaneously, the Syrians invaded the Golan Heights. After bitter fighting and heavy losses on both sides, the Israel Defence Forces were able to stem the Egyptian advance across the Sinai desert and to drive the Syrians out of the Golan Heights, pushing on to within 40 kilometres of Damascus. The Egyptians, however, remained entrenched in their positions on the east bank of the canal, though the Israeli forces, establishing a bridgehead across it, occupied an area to the west, effectively encircling the Egyptian Third Army.

On 22 October, the U.N. voted a cease-fire, and the war came to an end.

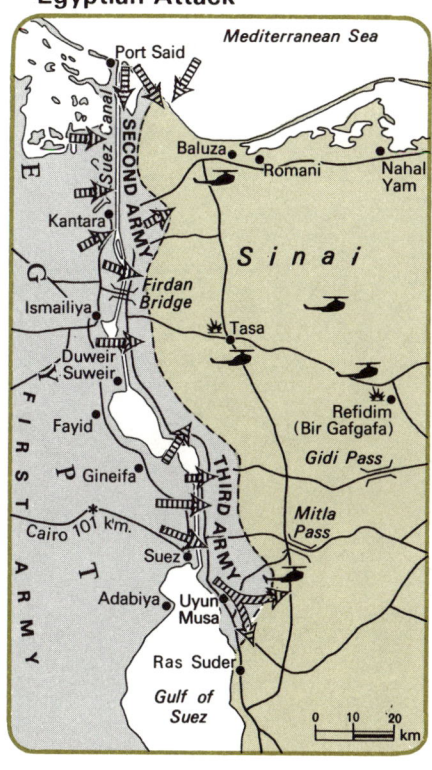

Egyptian Attack

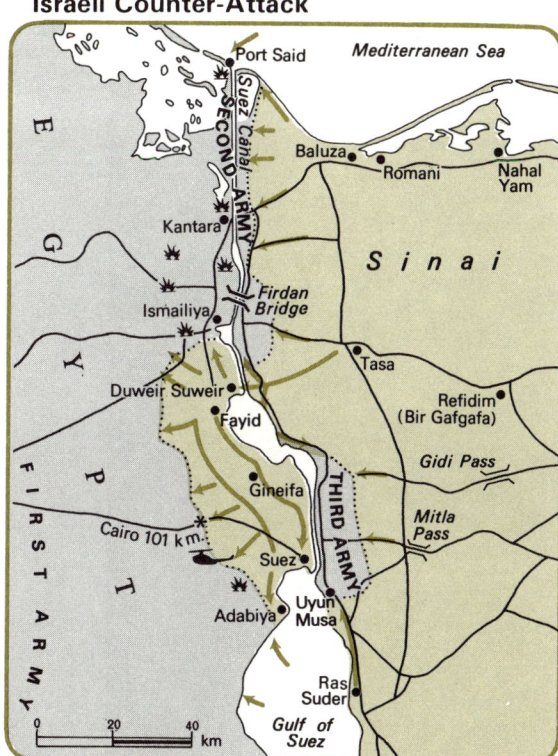

Israeli Counter-Attack

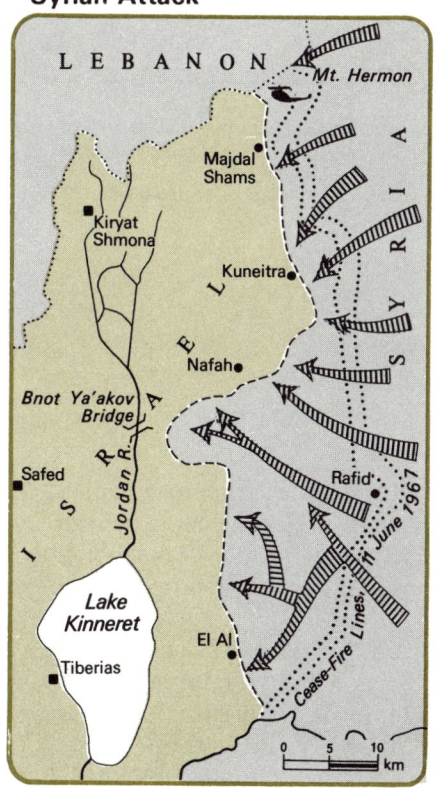

Syrian Attack

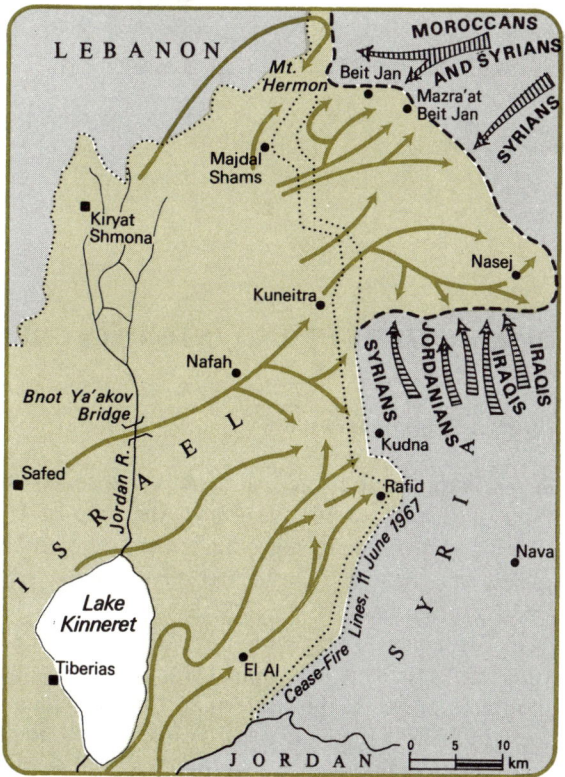

Israeli Counter-Attack

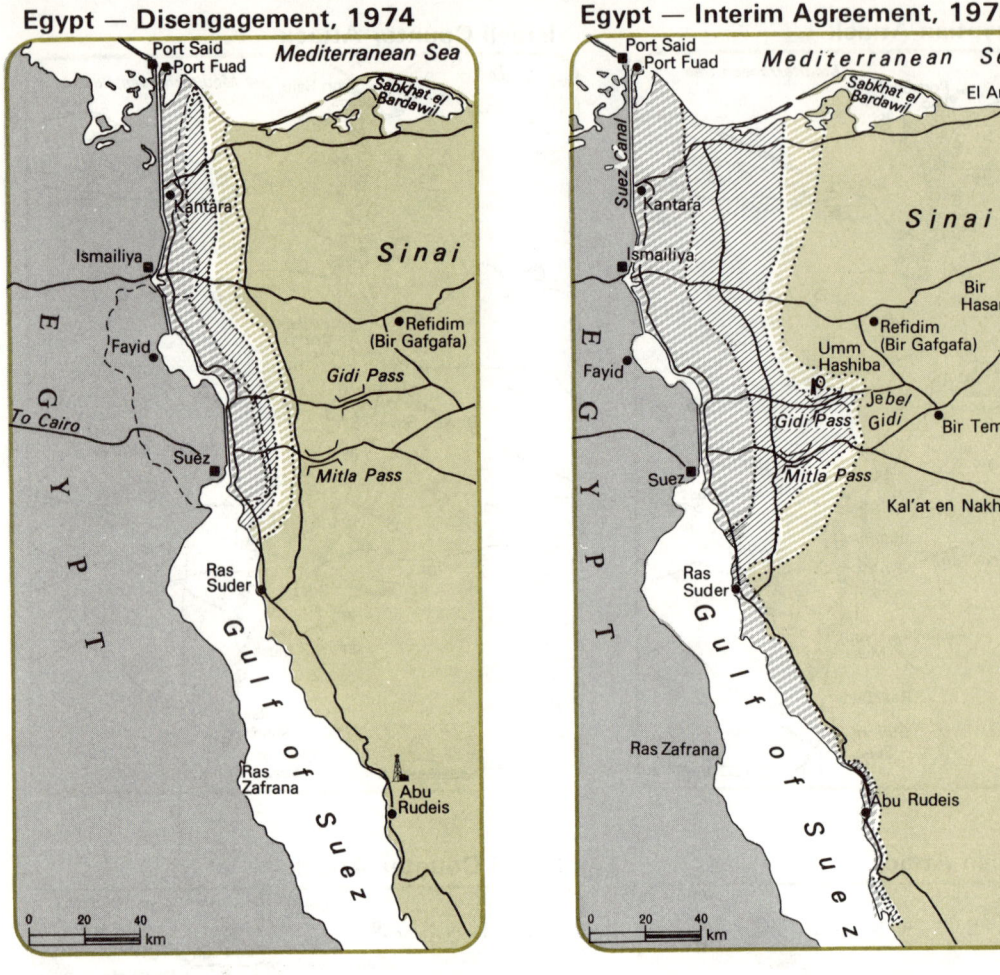

Israeli zone of limitation of forces
Egyptian zone of limitation of forces
U.N. Buffer zone
--- Extent of counter-attacks, Oct. 1973

DISENGAGEMENT AND INTERIM AGREEMENTS

Israel-Egypt Agreements

Several months after the cease-fire which ended the Yom Kippur War, the parties, in direct talks at Kilometre 101, and with the help of U.S. Secretary of State Henry Kissinger, concluded a disengagement agreement whereby the Israeli army withdrew eastward and pulled back from the Suez Canal to new lines. U.N. troops were introduced between Israeli and Egyptian lines.

In September 1975, with the assistance, once again, of Dr. Kissinger's diplomacy, an Interim Agreement was signed. Israel gave up part of Sinai, withdrawing from strategic mountain passes in the western part of the peninsula and from part of the Suez Gulf coast, including the Abu Rudeis oil fields. Egypt undertook to observe the cease-fire and to continue efforts aimed at negotiating a final peace settlement. It also promised that cargoes

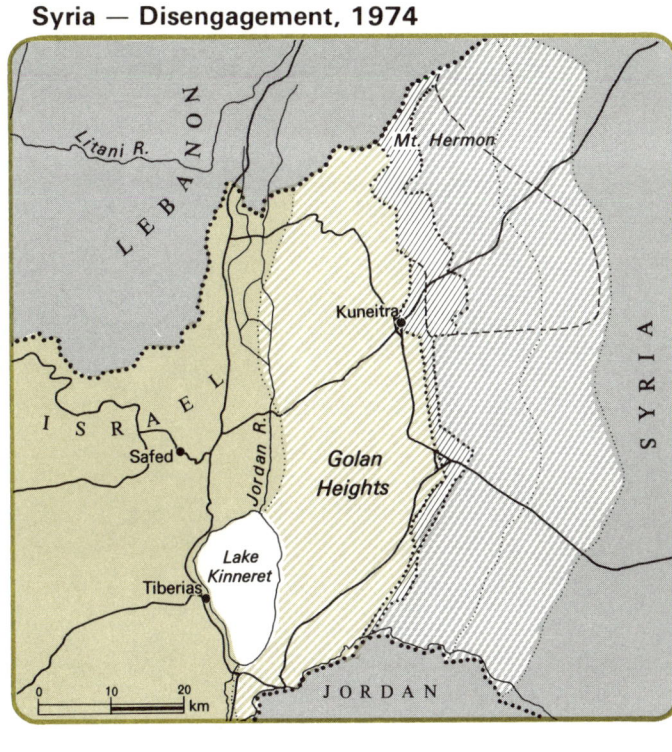

to and from Israel would be permitted to pass through the Suez Canal. Egyptian and Israeli surveillance stations were set up to prevent surprise attacks. By joint consent, the United States set up independent stations in the area.

Israel-Syria Disengagement (1974)

On the northern front at the end of the war, Israel held a large enclave in Syria. Eventually, a disengagement agreement was signed at the Geneva Peace Conference on 31 May 1974, with the Egyptians acting as proxies for the absent Syrians. Supervision of the agreement was placed in the hands of a U.N. Disengagement Observer Force (UNDOF), set up for this purpose by the Security Council. Though committed, under the agreement, to move towards a negotiated peace with Israel on the basis of Security Council Resolution 338, Syria refuses to recognize or to have any contact with Israel.

PEACE WITH EGYPT

Israeli-Egyptian relations, on the other hand, have taken a totally different turn. The Disengagement and Interim Agreements of 1974 and 1975, respectively, which grew out of the direct contacts at Kilometre 101 and Dr. Kissinger's "shuttle diplomacy" were destined to blossom, a few years later, into a full peace treaty — the first ever between Israel and an Arab state.

In November 1977, for the first time in three decades, an Arab leader responded positively to Israel's oft-repeated calls for a directly-negotiated peace settlement. Egypt's President Anwar Sadat made the historic journey to Jerusalem, where he was warmly welcomed, and where he conferred with Israeli Prime Minister Menachem Begin and other leaders and addressed the Knesset.

This was followed by a visit to Egypt by Prime Minister Begin in December and several more reciprocal visits in the years that followed. Negotiations began for a peace treaty between the two nations.

On 26 March 1979, the Egypt-Israel Peace Treaty was signed in Washington, D.C. by President Sadat and Prime Minister Begin, with President Jimmy Carter of the United States, who had played an active role in the negotiations, signing as a witness. The treaty provided for the normalization of relations between Egypt and Israel, including the exchange of ambassadors (which took place in February 1980), and Israel's withdrawal by April 1982, from all of the Sinai Peninsula.

For Israel, that meant relinquishing control of an area which had in the past served as a launching-pad for attacks against Israel. Israel also gave up a number of military and naval bases and several vital airfields, oilfields that had provided Israel with a large proportion of its energy needs, and a group of Jewish farming villages and a Jewish town that had been built during the previous decade — at a time when peace with Egypt was a distant dream.

Israel's Withdrawal from Sinai and Limited Forces Zones

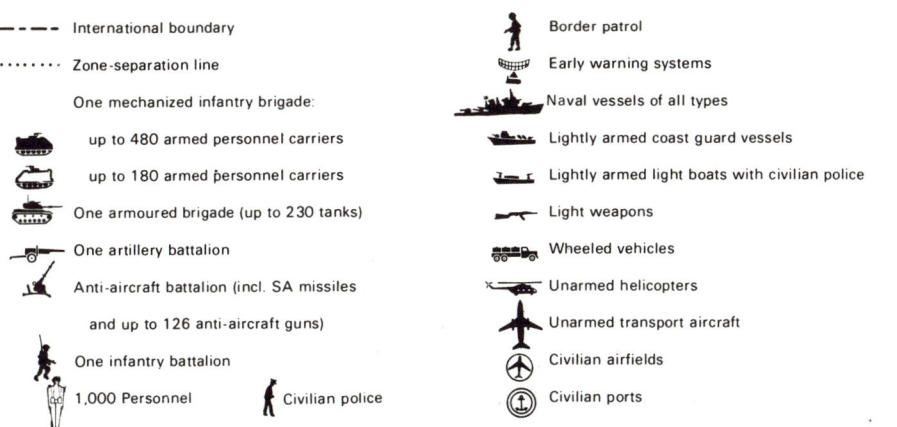

"PEACE FOR GALILEE" OPERATION 1982.

In order to distance the Palestine Liberation Organization who had set up a mini-military state in southern Lebanon from the civilian settlements of the Galilee, Israel embarked on a campaign against the P.L.O. on June 5th 1982.
 Fighting raged for more than two and a half months with Beirut besieged for several weeks. Repeated cease fires were arranged but these usually broke down some holding briefly for less than hours. With the effort of U.S. special enjoy Philip Habib, the first group of P.L.O. fighters trapped in the Lebanese capital began to evacuate Beirut on 22nd August — an evacuation which would take some fortnight to complete.
 In presidential elections held on August 24th, Bashir Jemayel, a Christian Falangist candidate, was democratically elected president of Lebanon. But on September 14th a bomb exploded in the Falangist headquarters in Beirut killing Mr. Jemayel. His brother Amin was then elected president.
 Peace talks were initiated on December 28th 1982 between Israel and Lebanon in the presence of United States representatives. Khalde in Lebanon and Kiryat Shmona in Israel were designated as the alternate sites for the talks.

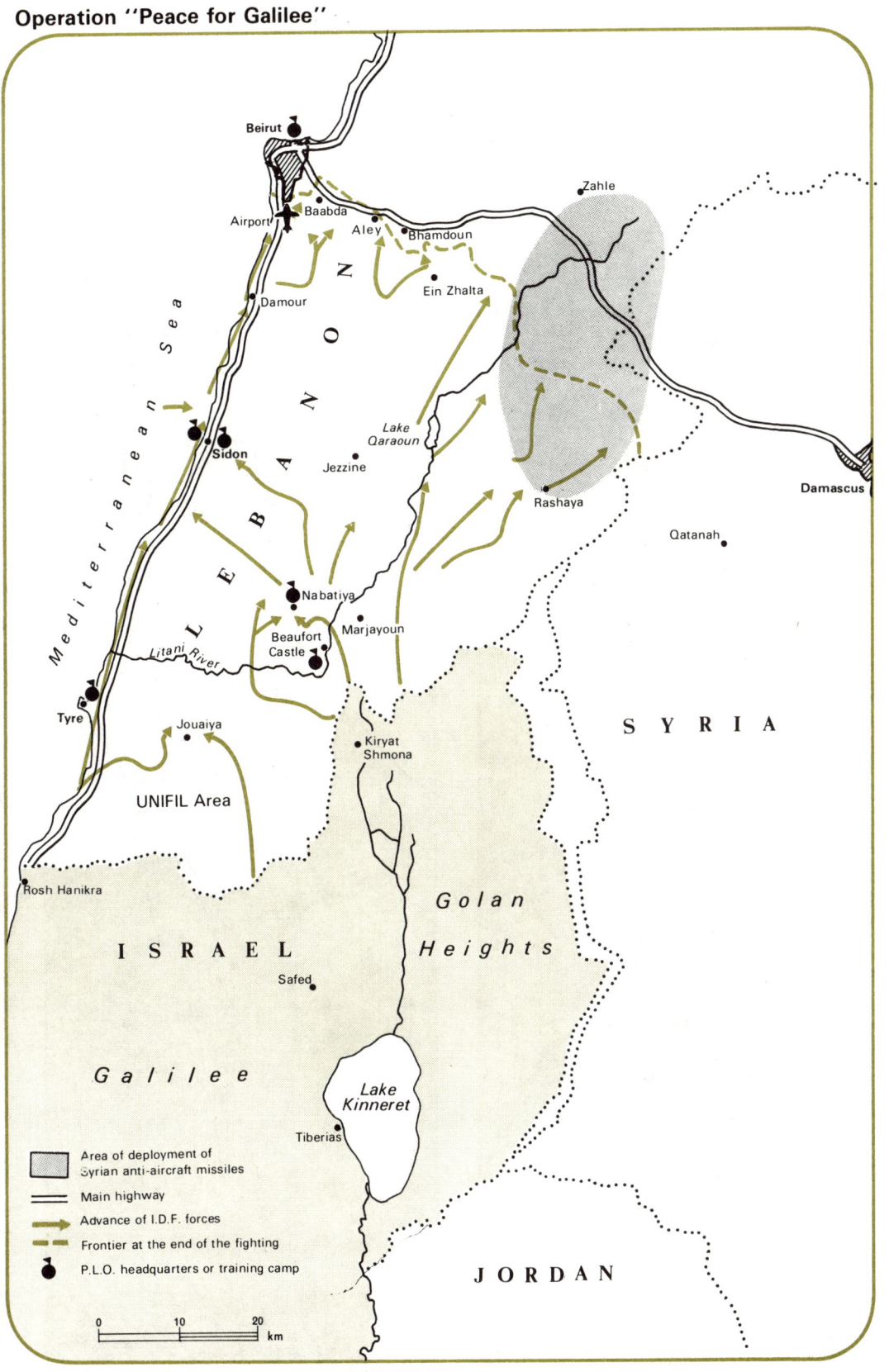

ISRAEL—TODAY

Topography

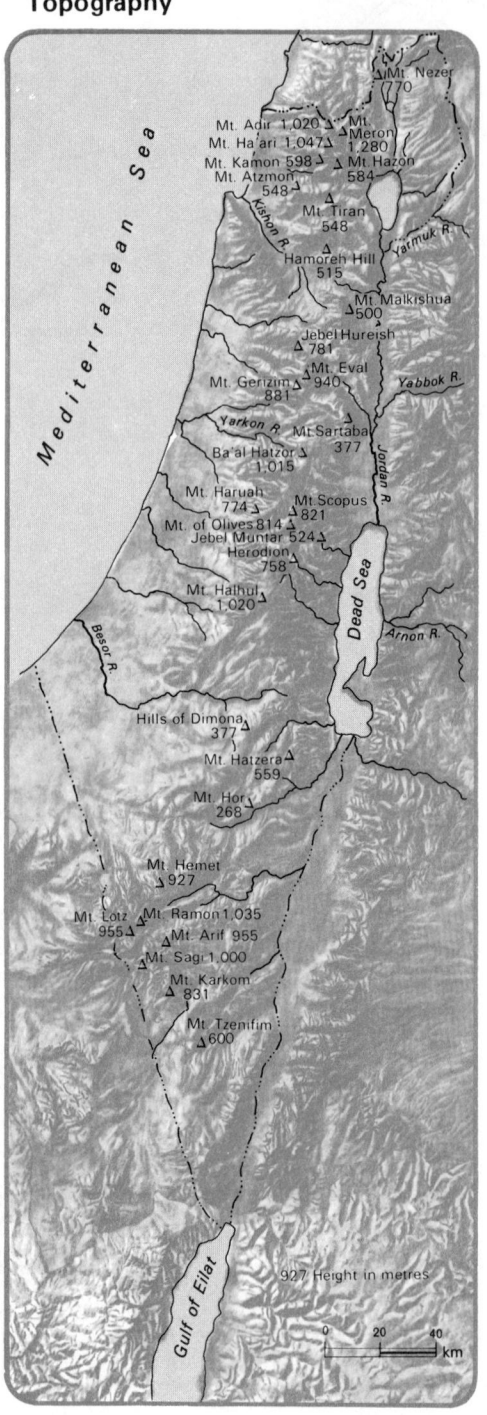

Geographical Regions

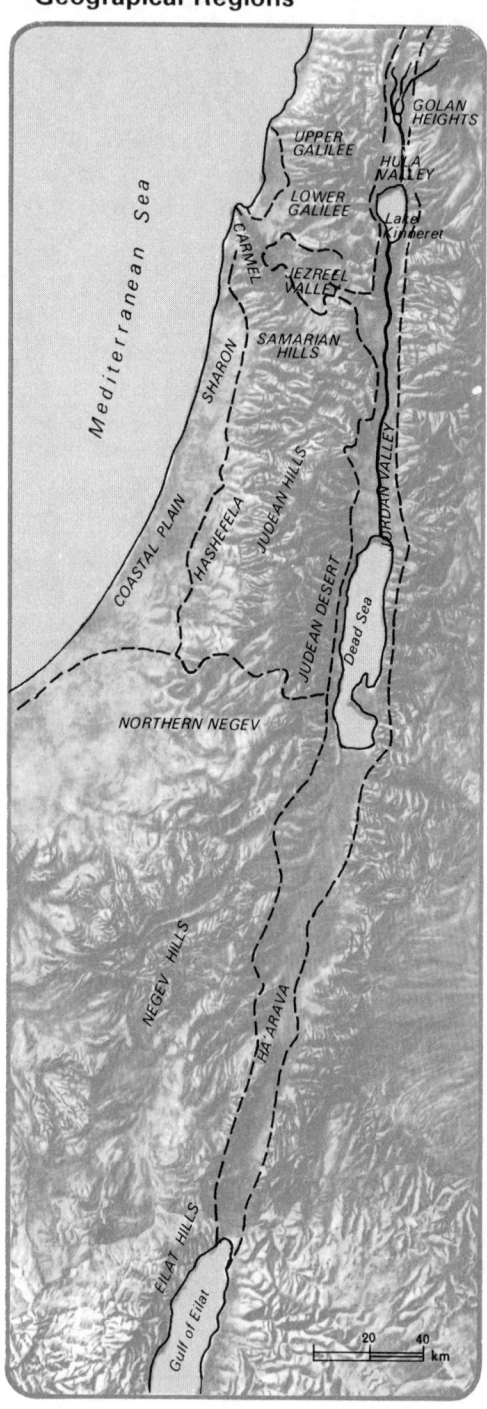

Summer Climate

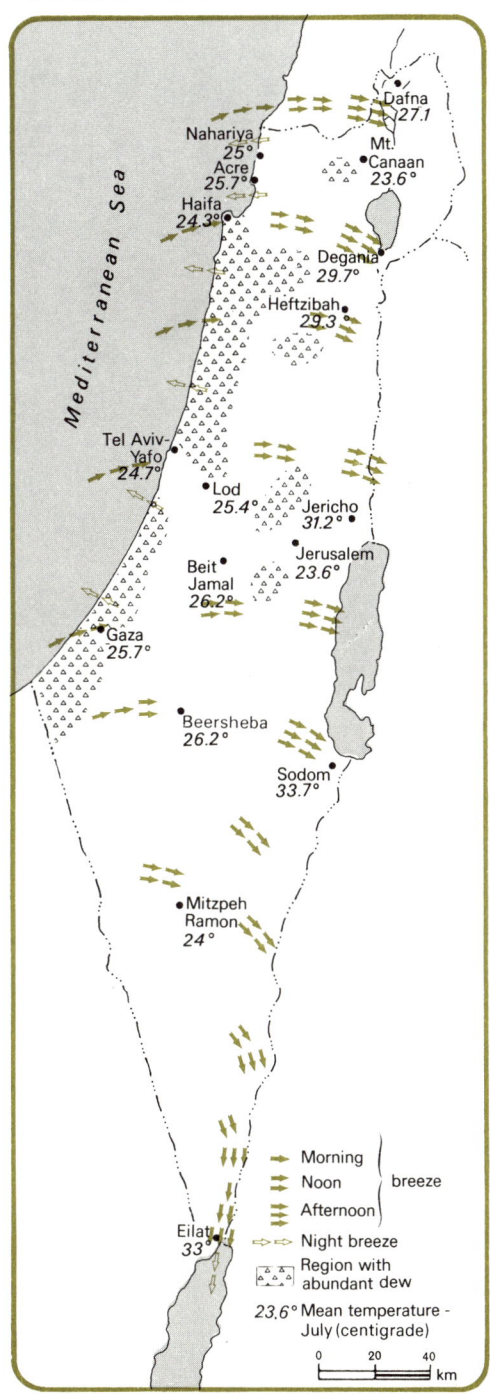

Winter Climate

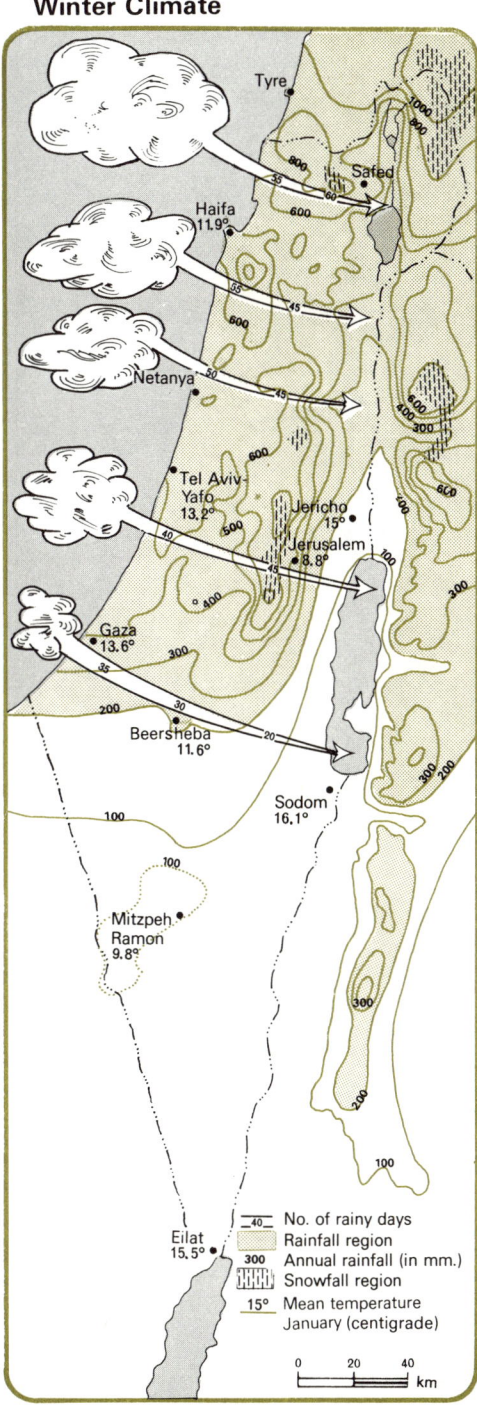

47

Rivers and Springs

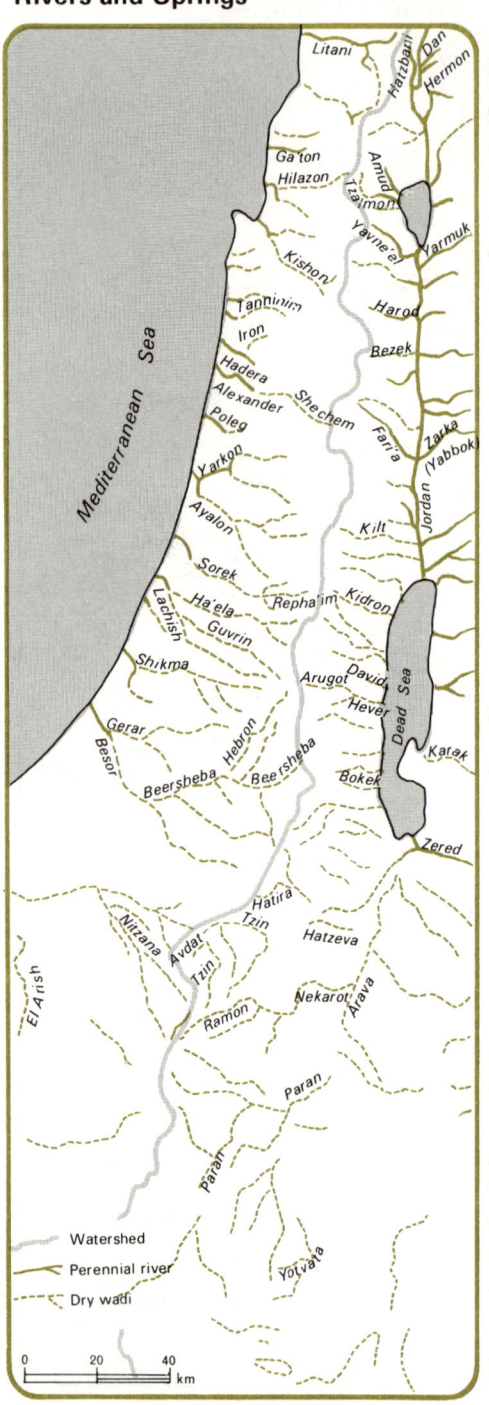

Vegetation

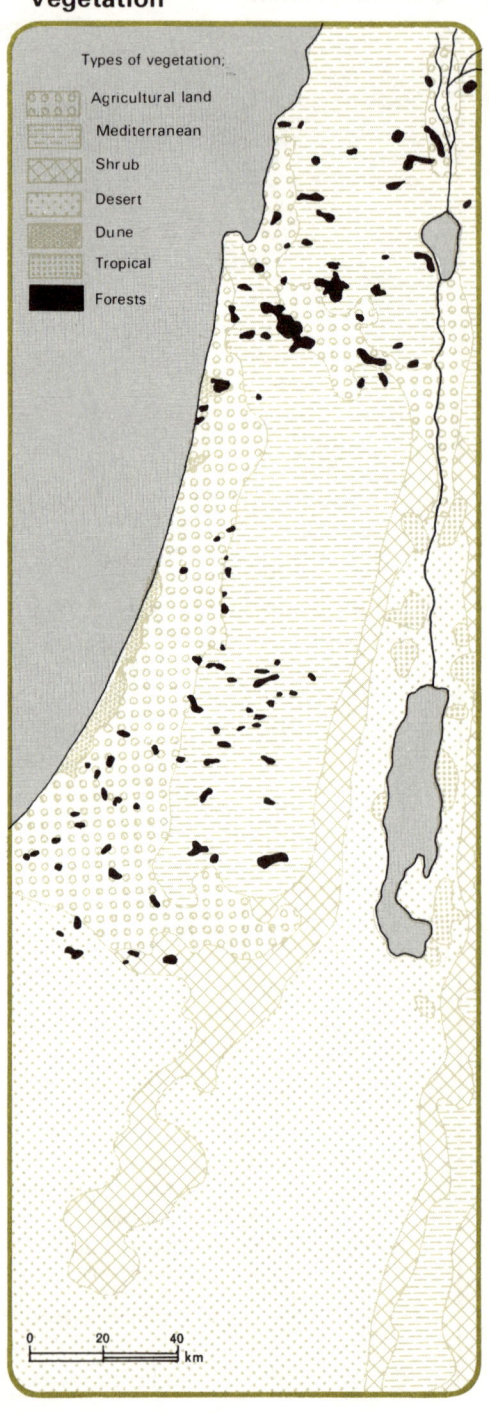

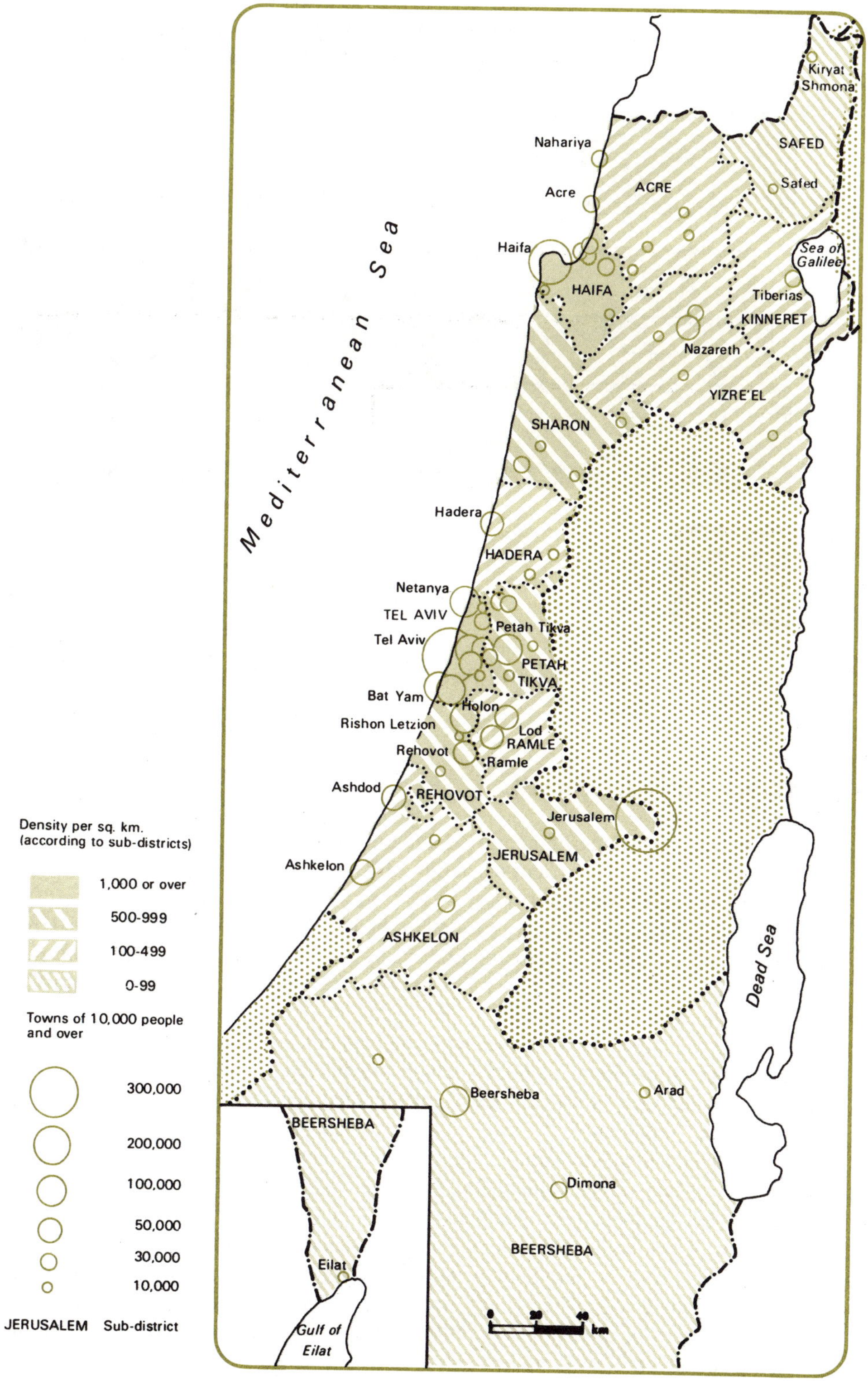

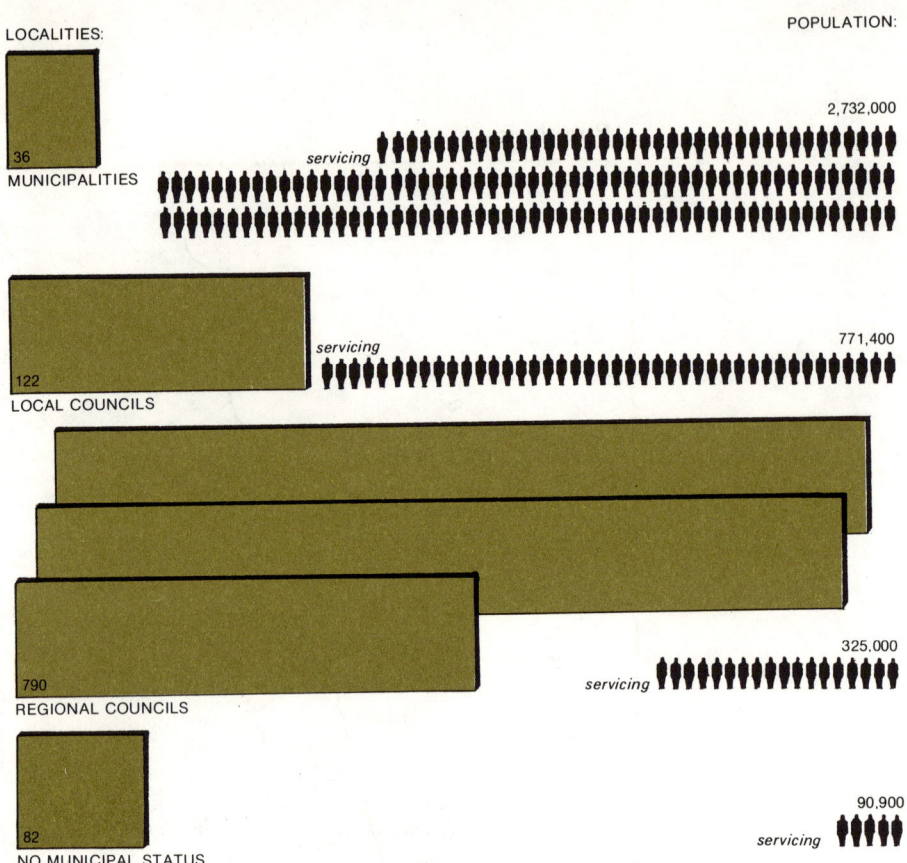

Localities and Population by Municipal Status

GOVERNMENT IN ISRAEL

The State of Israel is a parliamentary democracy with its capital in Jerusalem. In form it is a republic, headed by a President elected by the Knesset (Parliament) for a five-year period, renewable for one further period.

Supreme legislative authority is vested in the Knesset of 120 members elected by universal suffrage for a period of four years, under a system of proportional representation. Voters choose between national lists, seats being allocated in proportion to the number of votes obtained by each list.

Supreme executive authority lies with the Cabinet, headed by the Prime Minister. There are also local administrative bodies which are elected by proportional representation and provide services such as education and culture, health, sanitation, social welfare, water, road maintenance, parks, etc.

The Judiciary is by law completely independent of government and Knesset control: it is divided into Magistrates' Courts, District Courts and the Supreme Court. Religious Courts have jurisdiction in certain matters of personal status, such as marriage.

The State Comptroller keeps watch on the efficiency, economy and ethical integrity of the public services and of public corporations in the management or financing of which the government has a share. He is appointed for five years (renewable) by the President, on recommendation of a Knesset committee, and is responsible to the Knesset alone; he also functions as an ombudsman.

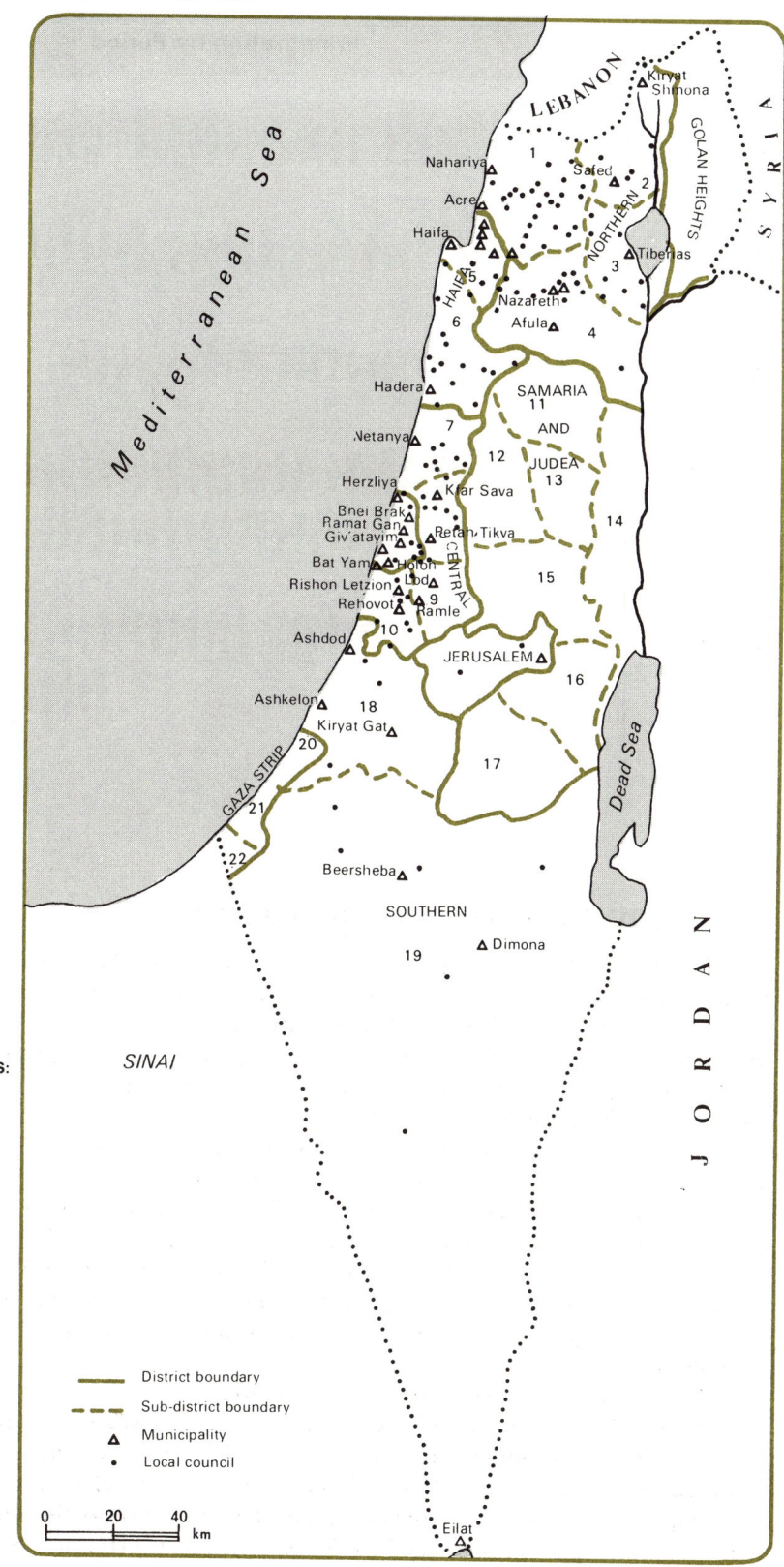

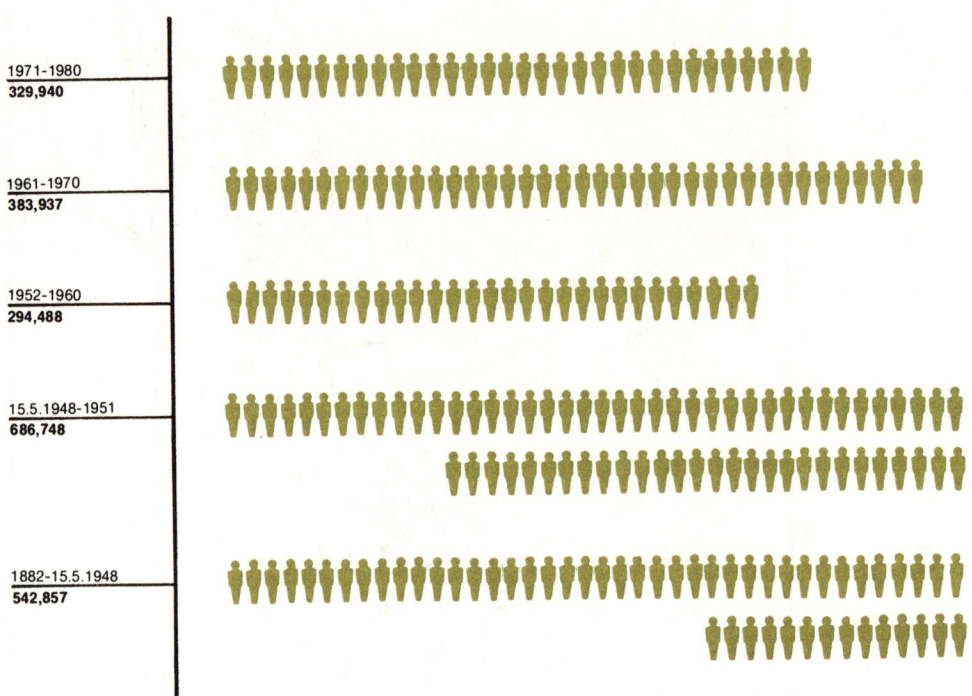

ALIYAH (IMMIGRATION) AND ABSORPTION

The government of the newly established state of Israel in 1948 made it its first order of business to open the gates of the Jewish state wide for any Jew from any part of the world who sought the haven of Israel's shores. The Law of Return grants immediate Israeli citizenship to every Jewish immigrant. Other immigrants may also obtain Israeli citizenship but they are required to undergo the customary process of naturalization. (Israel's 2,450,000 citizens-by-birth include nearly 600,000 Arabs.)

Since 1948, some 1,700,000 Jews have come to the country, most of them refugees from war-torn Europe, as well as about 700,000 refugees from Arab countries. Well over half a million came within the first four years of Israel's statehood. This large wave of immigration was mainly the result of persecution. Today's immigration is usually voluntary. In recent years there have been more arrivals from the affluent countries of the West. An unexpected and welcome development, following the Six-Day War, was an influx of immigrants from the Soviet Union, though here numbers vary depending on the twists and turns of Soviet emigration policy.

The newcomers are assisted in obtaining housing and jobs and other facilities, after passing through absorption centres administered by the government and the Jewish Agency. Often, on arrival, the immigrants need to be retrained for new professions.

A network of "development towns" has been created throughout the country to absorb the immigrants socially and economically, and integrate them into the life of the nation. In many cases, integration is speeded by hostels and *ulpanim* (Hebrew classes).

Immigrant Absorption

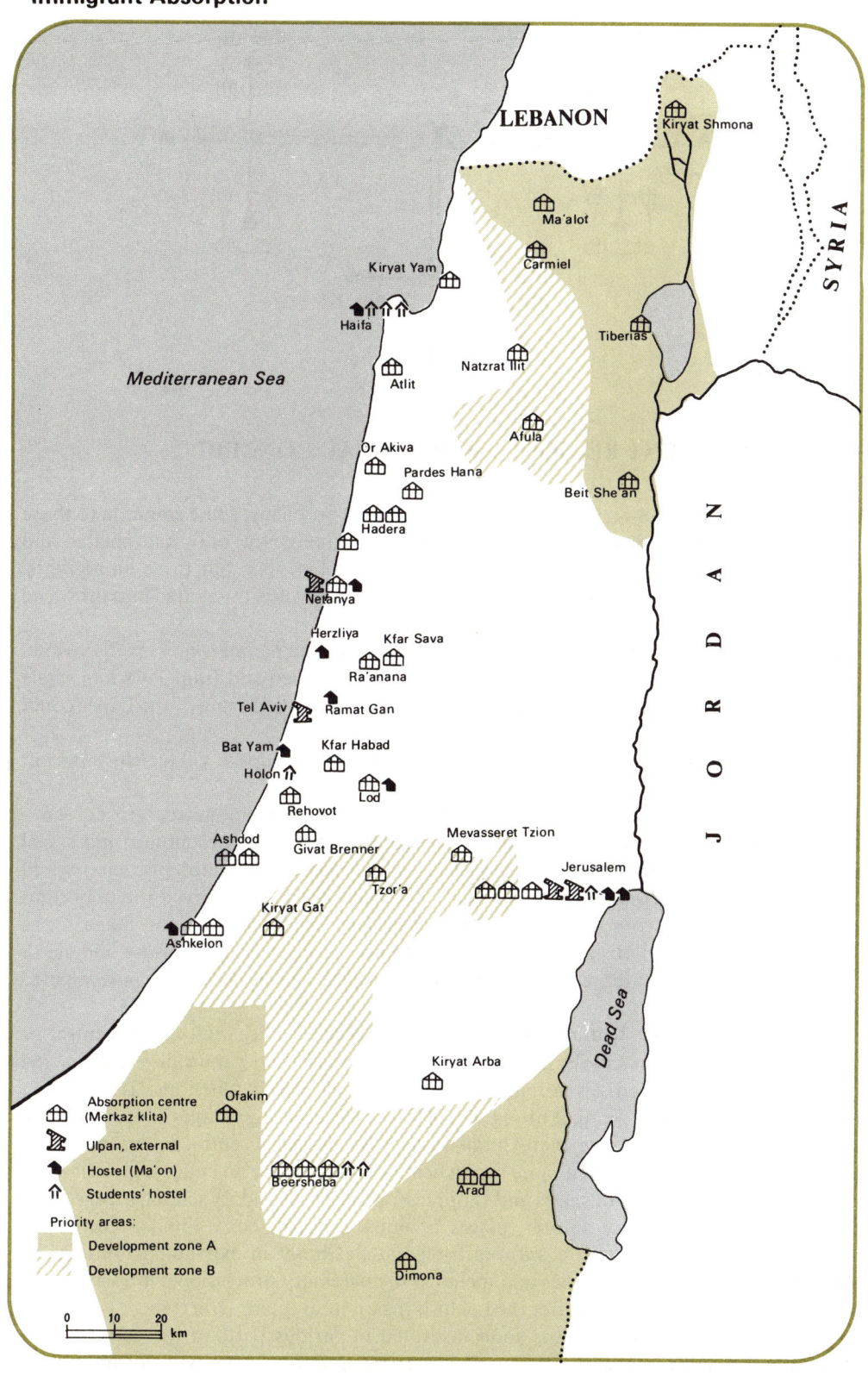

The Lachish Plan

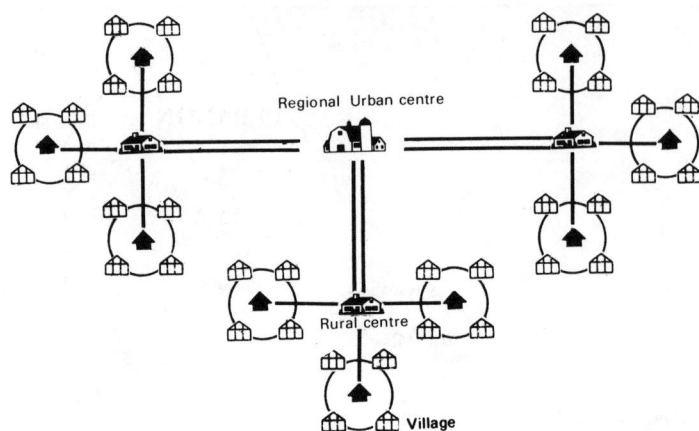

THE DEVELOPMENT REGION: A NEW SOCIAL CONCEPT

Mass immigration over a very short span of time created problems, some common to those of other immigrant societies and others unique to Israel. Not only had shelter and subsistence to be provided for hundreds of thousands of people, but these immigrants, coming from very different cultural backgrounds, had to be swiftly integrated into the social and economic fabric of modern Israel.

The "melting-pot" concept was first tried and failed. Israeli planners quickly discovered that they could not throw together Tunisian, Polish, Moroccan and Iraqi Jews in a single village and expect them all to get along with each other. The Ingathering of the Exiles could hardly be achieved by such "pressure-cooker" methods.

From this negative experience emerged the Lachish Plan: groups of village-clusters built around centrally located urban centres or development towns.

A cluster would comprise four or five demographically homogeneous or semi-homogeneous villages grouped around a local rural centre, where economic and social facilities (shops, mechanical repair station, elementary school, clinic, clubhouse, etc.) would be available for all the villages in the cluster. The rural centre also served the important function of breaking down social barriers by offering Jews from "the Tunisian village", "the Iraqi village" and "the Polish village" the opportunity to meet at their leisure and get to know each other. Moreover, children from varied origins and backgrounds now went to school together.

A little later, another feature was added to the plan: the regional urban centre, or development town. Situated at the geographic centre of five or more rural village-clusters, the regional centre performed several major economic and social functions. Its factories processed the agricultural produce brought in from the surrounding villages and, at the same time, provided employment for many immigrants. Like the rural centre, the urban centre offers services and facilities, on a more sophisticated level, to serve an entire region (it has a greater number and variety of shops and shopping centres, a secondary school, a large clinic or medical centre, a police station, places of entertainment, etc.). Finally, the urban character of the regional centre allowed for great flexibility in expanding housing for immigrant as well as other families and included the necessary professional infrastructure.

The Lachish Plan (so named after the Lachish region in southern Israel where it was first applied) proved a success and was soon instituted in various parts of the country — a welcome and practical answer to Israel's most pressing needs in the fields of immigrant absorption and general economic development.

Development Towns and Local Centres

55

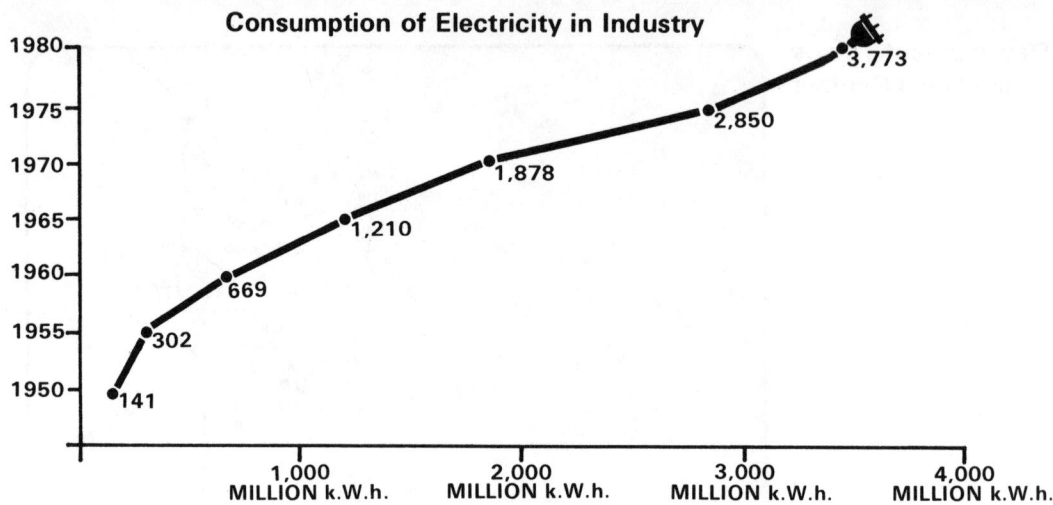

ECONOMIC DEVELOPMENT AND INDUSTRY

Not many years ago, Israel was classed among the underdeveloped countries. Today it finds itself in the developed category — with good reason. Its economic advancement has been exceptional. From 1950 to 1980 the gross national product increased more than tenfold.

The economic dislocations that have plagued the world over the past decade, resulting in large part from frequent and often unpredictable oil price hikes since 1971, have had their impact on the Israeli economy too. Israel, however, has its own special economic problems. The economy has to shoulder the heavy burden of defence expenditure. Moreover, Israel all along has had to face the challenge of absorbing large numbers of immigrants of various backgrounds and of providing them with suitable housing and employment. Many of them have come from technologically primitive societies and need to be trained for living in a modern environment.

Israel's agriculture is highly advanced, yet much of the land still remains to be brought under cultivation. Since 1948, when Israel became independent, the area of land under cultivation has increased from 408,000 acres to 1,075,000 acres. The country has aimed, as far as possible, for agricultural self-sufficiency, which to a large extent has been attained. Because of limited rainfall, however, the development of agriculture is very much dependent on irrigation.

Much effort has been invested in Israel over the years in developing more efficient irrigation systems. One highly successful result has been the drip irrigation technique — now in wide use throughout Israel and all over the world. Computerized irrigation (and fertilization) is today coming into its own in Israel, offering significant savings not only in precious water, but in time and labour. Between 1948 and 1981, the area under irrigation has increased from 75,000 to over 500,000 acres.

Citrus fruit is the chief agricultural export, but the cultivation of fruit, flowers and vegetables for the off-season European market is also highly developed.

Industry, likewise, has grown rapidly. Since the domestic market is limited, industrial development has depended on exports. Most raw materials being scarce in Israel, industry has concentrated on enterprises of science and technology. A handful of electronic, computer and science-based industries are now in the forefront of supplying equipment to the ever-advancing world market. Israel is one of the world's largest exporters of polished industrial diamonds; other major exports include textiles, fashions, chemical products and processed foodstuffs.

Industry and Development

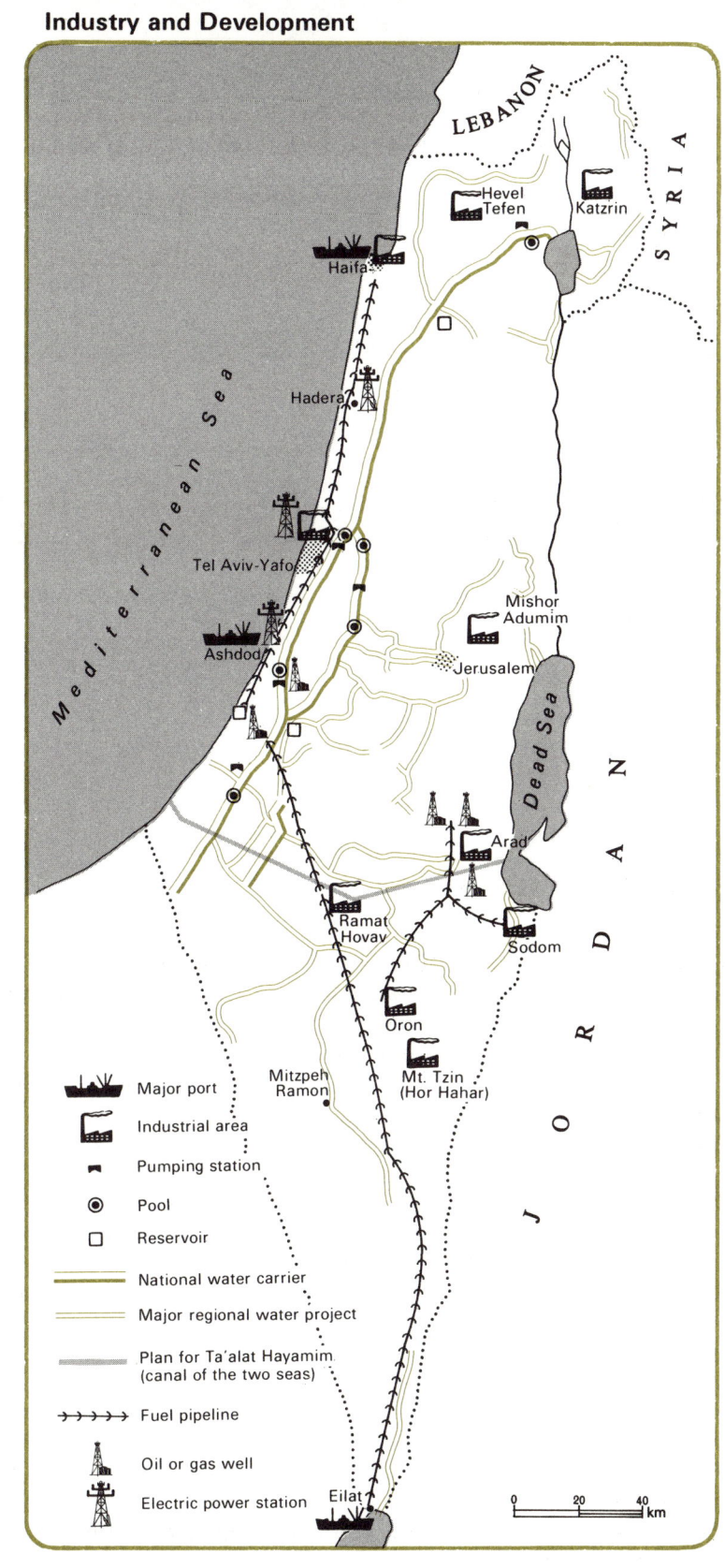

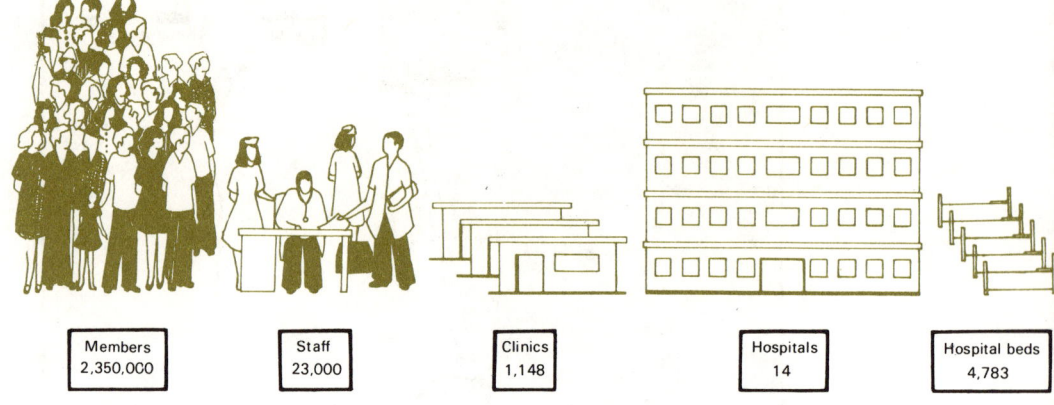

LABOUR MOVEMENTS

Self-help has always been a cardinal principle for the workers of Israel. Their labour unions have therefore been much more than trade unions in the ordinary sense of the term; they have also, for instance, founded their own industrial enterprises, transport cooperatives, banks insurance companies, pension funds, cultural institutions, newspapers, health services, construction companies, supermarkets and sports organizations, etc.

A large part of Israel's agricultural production comes from the *kibbutzim* (communal farms) and *moshavim* (co-operative villages) organized in country-wide associations affiliated to the labour organizations. Koor, the major Histadrut industrial concern, is listed among the world's largest.

There are four main labour organizations:
1. The Histadrut (General Federation of Labour), which is open to Druze and Arab workers as well as Jews. It has over 1,250,000 adult members. The Histadrut provides numerous amenities such as its sick fund (the Kupat Holim) and the Hapo'el sports organization. Among Histadrut affiliates are the Solel Boneh (Building and Public Works Co.), Tnuva (Agricultural Marketing Cooperative) and Hamashbir Hamerkazi (Cooperative Wholesale Society).
2. Hapo'el Hamizrahi (Religious Workers' Cooperative). It has 105,000 members and 71 affiliated villages (11 *kibbutzim* and 60 *moshavim*).
3. Histadrut Ha'ovdim Hale'umit (National Labour Federation). It has 80,000 members and 13 affiliated villages.
4. Po'alei Agudat Israel (Orthodox Workers' Cooperative). It has 16,000 adult members and 17 affiliated villages.

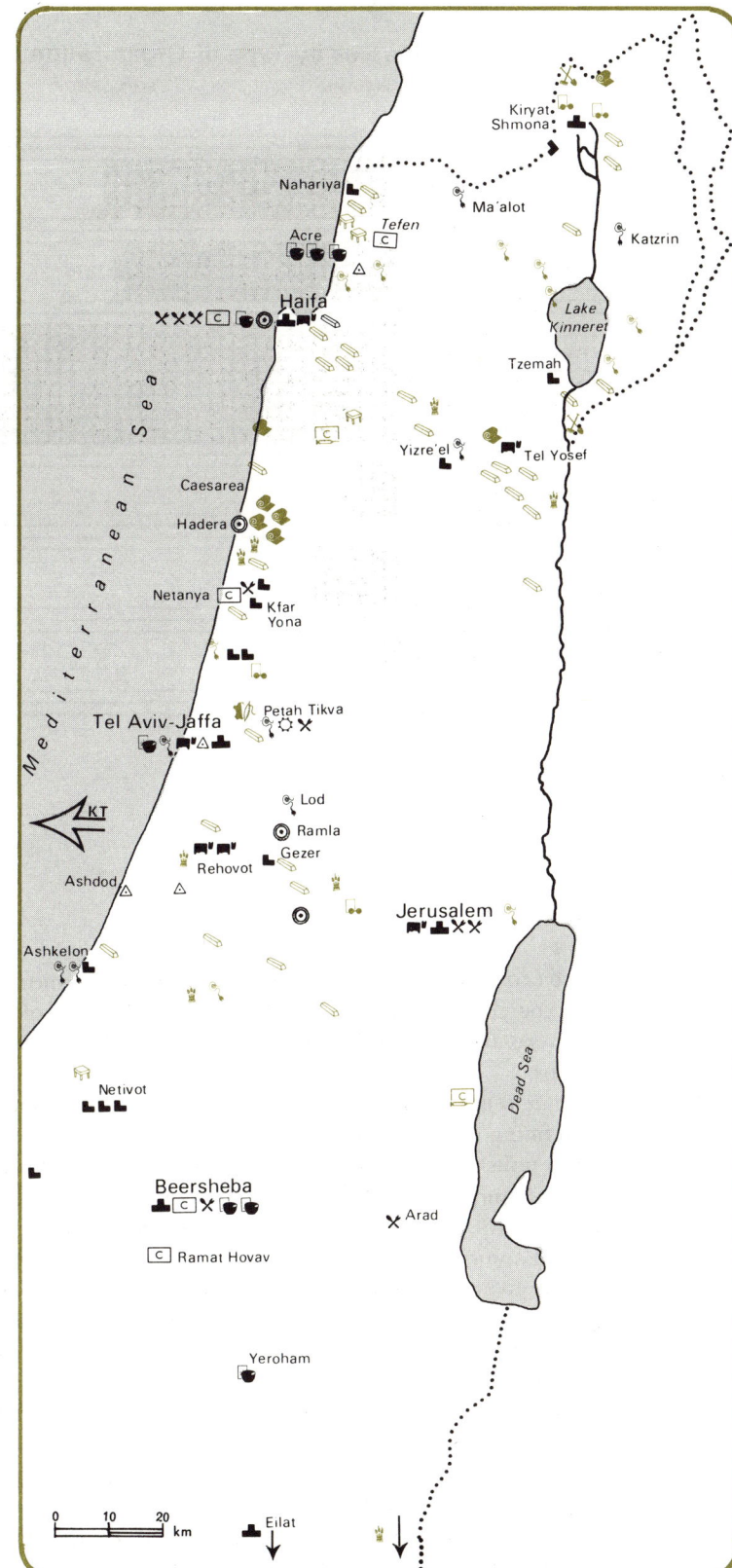

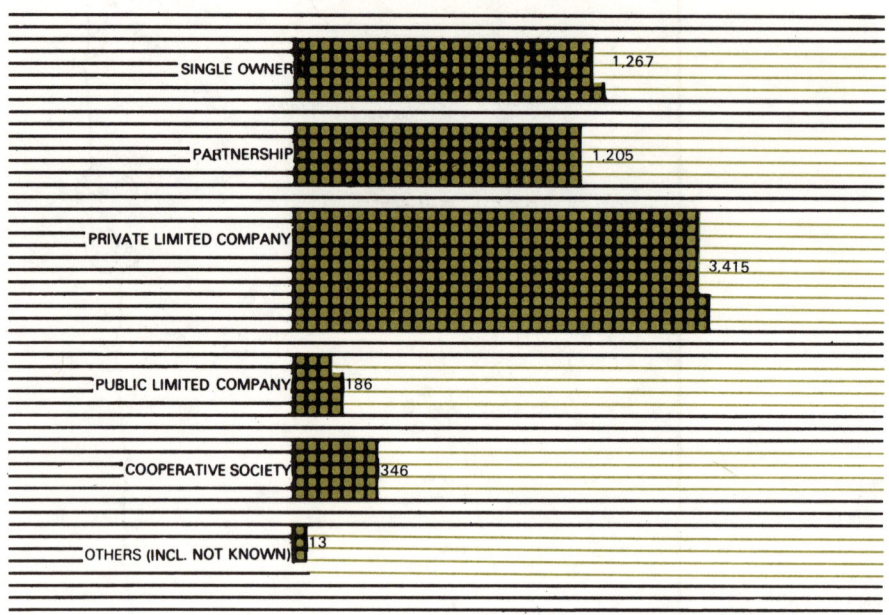

PRIVATE ENTERPRISE

Israel has a mixed economy. The vast majority of enterprises — more than 90 percent — are privately owned; 5 percent are owned by the Histadrut (Federation of Labour) and less than 3 percent by the government. On the other hand, less than half of the labour force is employed in private concerns.

Naturally enough, it is some of the publicly owned industries — such as mining, chemicals and petroleum refining — that require some of the heaviest capital outlays. On the other hand, the cut and polished industrial diamond industry — Israel's largest single export in terms of value — is mostly privately owned. Privately owned agriculture, mostly citrus plantations, accounts for over 32 percent of labour in that branch of production. In many industries, two and sometimes all three forms of ownership are represented.

The government gives considerable encouragement to private investors by way of low-cost, long-term loans, tax reductions, customs protection, provision of premises, etc. The Tourist Development corporation assists particularly in the private development of hotels, restaurants and transport.

Under the Law for the Encouragement of Capital Investment, designed particularly for enterprises with foreign capital or for those producing goods for export, very considerable facilities and privileges are granted. These include development loans, assistance in land purchase, site development and construction in development areas, loans for working capital, special depreciation allowances, exemption from customs and purchase tax on equipment, and income and property tax concessions.

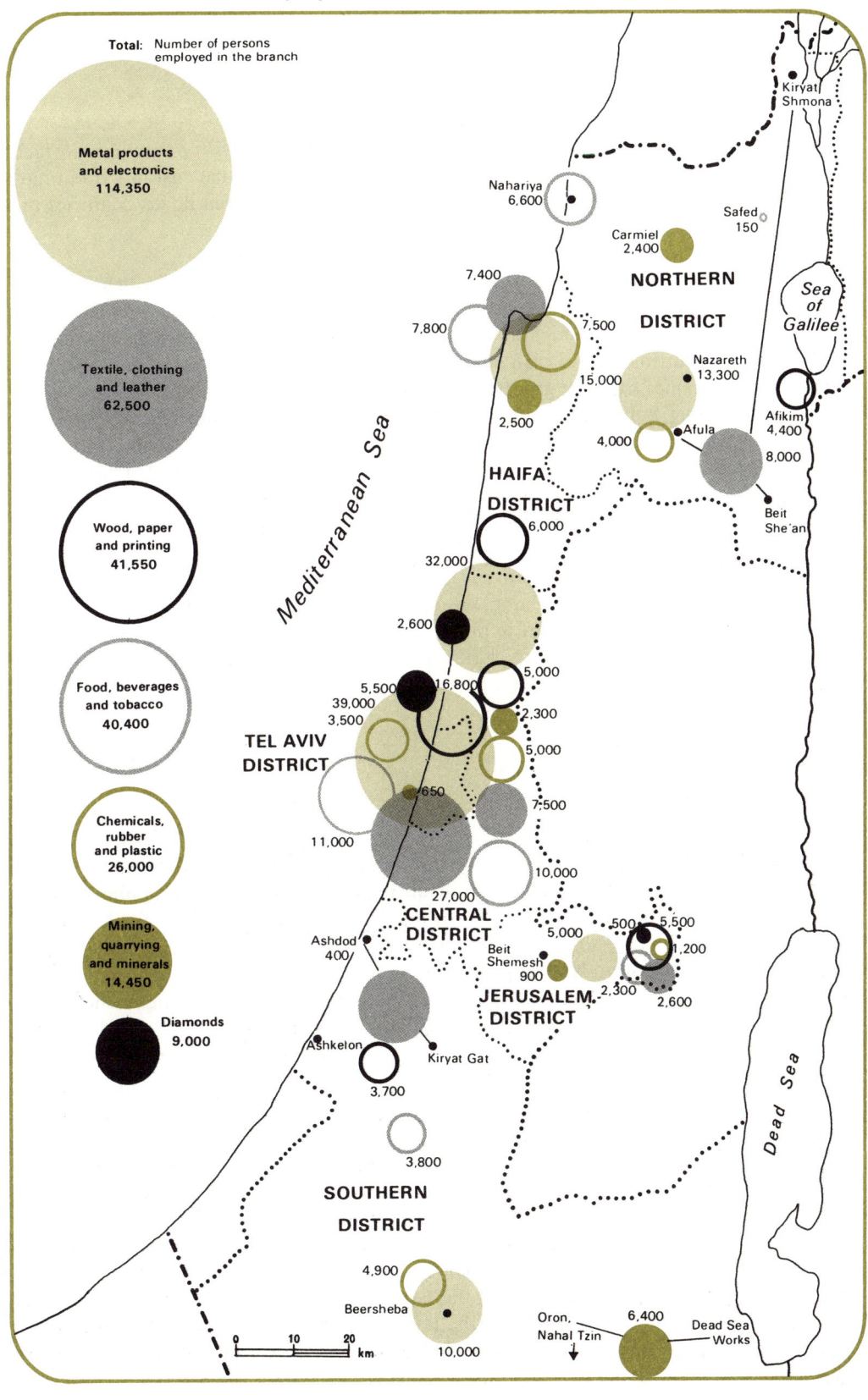

COMMUNITIES

Jewish Communities

The "Ingathering of the Exiles" has brought into modern Israel Jewish communities which in the many centuries of dispersion have developed their own particular customs, traditions, life-patterns and ethnic characteristics. They come from some seven dozen countries the world over.

There is space here to describe only a few of these communities.

The Yemenites lived in isolation for centuries in southwestern Arabia which rendered them uniquely suited to preserve their Hebrew and religious tradition. They are noted for their contribution to Israel's religious literature and poetry, for their dance-groups and for their exquisite gold filigree work. In Meah Shearim and nearby quarters of Jerusalem are concentrated extreme Orthodox groups originating in Eastern Europe and still dressed in the garb of 17th-century Poland; many of them use Yiddish as their daily language, Hebrew being reserved for prayer only. The Moroccan Jews have brought with them a colourful set of family ceremonial customs, as well as some folk festivals that have attracted nationwide attention and widespread participation. The Samaritans are an ancient people related to the Jews and residing in the mountains of Samaria. They hold only the first part of the Bible (the Five Books of Moses and the Book of Joshua) to be sacred. The high point of their religious calendar is the Passover festival, when they gather on Mount Gerizim, overlooking Shechem (Nablus), to offer up the paschal lamb, exactly as prescribed in the Bible.

There has been a conscious effort to preserve the special cultural and folk traditions that each community has brought with it to Israel. The variety of these traditions adds colour and a human richness to the Israeli cultural scene.

Arab and Other Communities

The Arab community in Israel proper has grown rapidly since 1949, when it stood at a little over 150,000, to more than 600,000 today. Arab Israelis are free to maintain and promote their own culture, tradition and language. Arabic is one of Israel's two official languages.

Arabs and Druze play an active role in Israel's political life, with a voter participation rate consistently running well over 80 percent (substantially better than among Israel's Jews). Representatives of both communities have been elected to all Knessets. Today, more than 350,000 Arabs live in cities, while a quarter-million populate some one hundred villages.

Israel's 50,000 semi-nomadic Bedouin retain their age-old way of life, though a growing number are availing themselves of the facilities and services offered by modern society. Some serve voluntarily in Israel's army or border police; many have abandoned the life of the nomad to settle down in permanent homes in town or village.

Arab women have begun to perform a more active role in society. Their status has risen as a result of Israel's social legislation, which abolished polygamy and child marriage, granting women full voting rights and instituted free and compulsory education for girls.

The Druze, a breakaway group from Islam, live mainly in Galilee and the Golan Heights. Their religion is a secret, and if you ask them why, they will answer: that, too, is a secret. At their own request, Druze youth serve in the Israel Defence Forces.

Another minority group in Israel are the Bahais, whose world centre is in Haifa. Their gold-domed temple and surrounding Persian Gardens on the slopes of Mount Carmel are one of the tourist attractions of that city.

Ethnic Communities

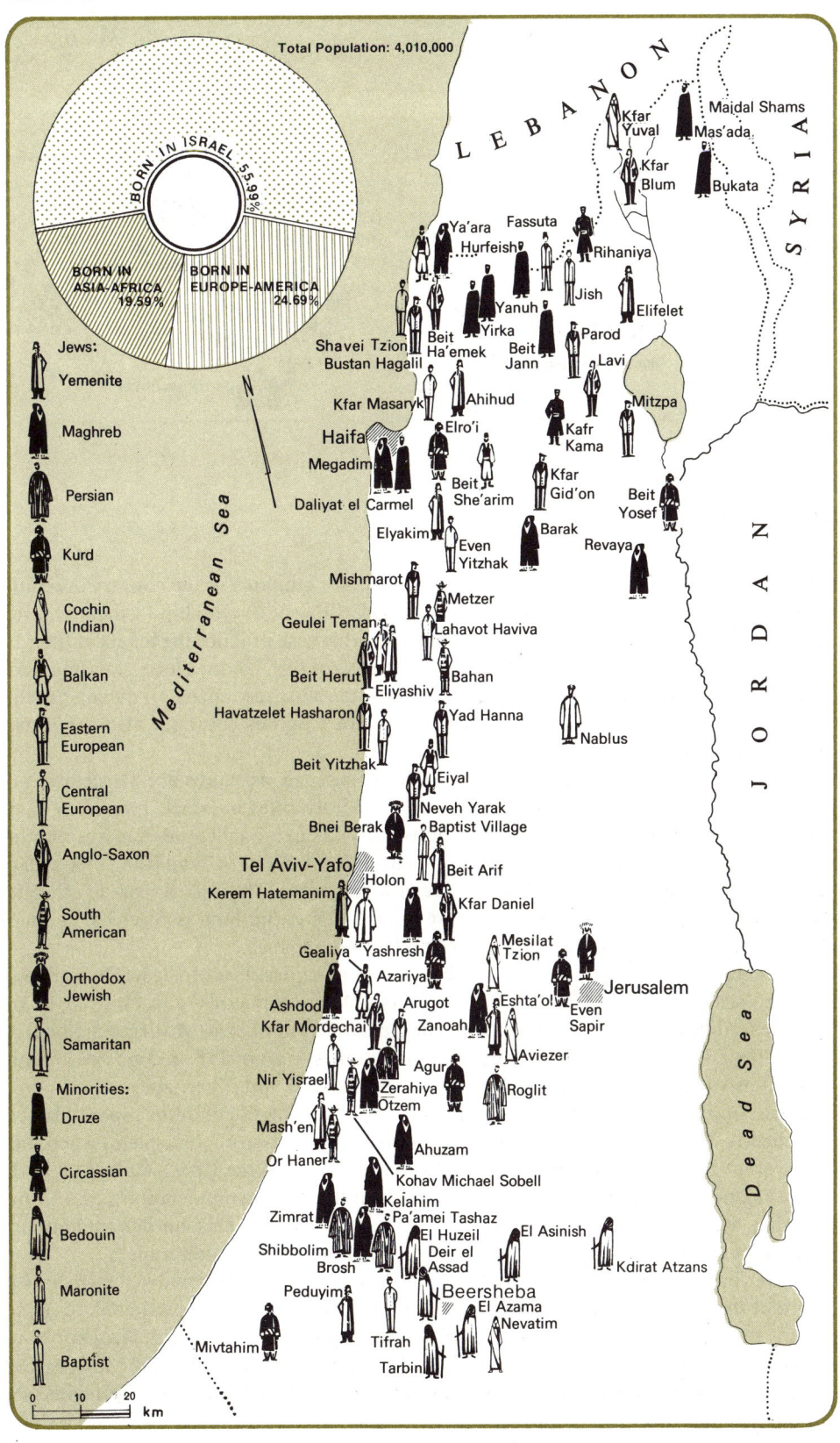

Holy Places of Jerusalem

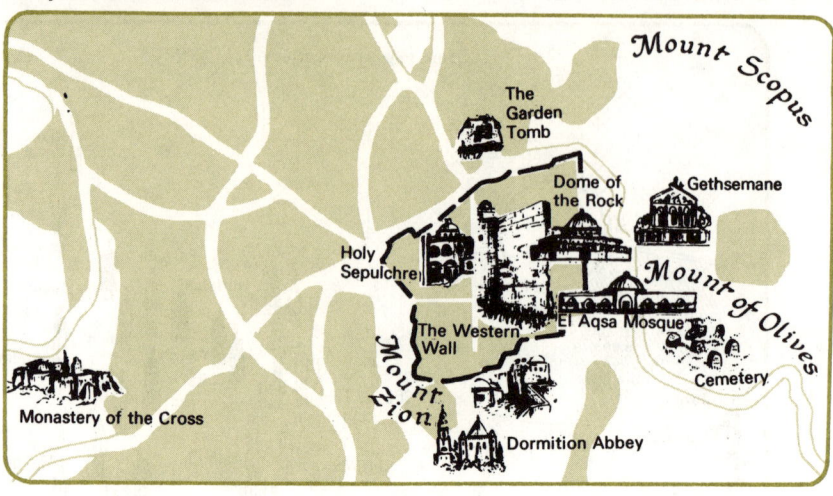

RELIGIOUS LIFE

There is no official religion in Israel. The three main religions in the country are Judaism, Islam and Christianity, and their adherents are at liberty to worship in their accustomed traditions, maintain their places of worship and otherwise practice the tenets of their faiths, including the observance of their holy days and days of rest. Under a long-standing tradition that pre-dates the independence of Israel in 1948, the state recognizes all the major religions and, in matters of personal status, their respective religious courts; it also supports their institutions out of the state budget.

The majority of Israel's inhabitants are Jews; most of its Arabs are Moslems.

Down the centuries, Judaism has revered four holy cities in Israel: Jerusalem, Hebron, Tiberias and Safed. Jerusalem — for a thousand years in biblical times and again today the capital of Israel — is the most sacred, and within it the Western Wall (the outer wall of the Temple Compound) is the focal point of Jewish sentiment. There are a score of other Jewish holy places in the country, but, in point of fact, the entire land is regarded as sacred in Jewish law and tradition. There are some 6,000 synagogues.

Islam has 19 holy places and over one hundred mosques. For Moslems, Jerusalem is the third holiest city, after Mecca and Medina, its golden Dome of the Rock being linked, in Islamic tradition, with Mohammed's "night journey". The Sharia (Moslem religious) courts — like their Jewish counterparts, the rabbinical courts — enjoy fully recognized jurisdiction in matters of personal status, such as marriage, divorce and inheritance.

Christianity venerates the country as the setting for the life of Jesus. Special sanctity is attached to Bethlehem, his birthplace (Church of the Nativity); Jerusalem, where he died (Church of the Holy Sepulchre, Via Dolorosa, Stations of the Cross, Calvary, Garden of Gethsemane); Nazareth, where he grew up (Church of the Annunciation); and Cana and Tabgha, where he performed miracles. There are some 30 Christian denominations, 300 churches and chapels, and over 2,000 clergy, including monks and nuns.

The Druze, who broke away from Islam at the end of the tenth century, live mainly in the north of the country (Galilee and Golan). Since their religion is a closed book to outsiders, little is known of its tenets or practices. The Druze claim descent from Jethro, father-in-law of Moses, and their chief holy site is Jethro's Tomb, Nebi Shu'eib, in the hills of Galilee.

The Bahai faith, a more recent offshoot of Islam, is centred in Israel: its principal shrines are in Acre and Haifa.

Holy Sites in Israel

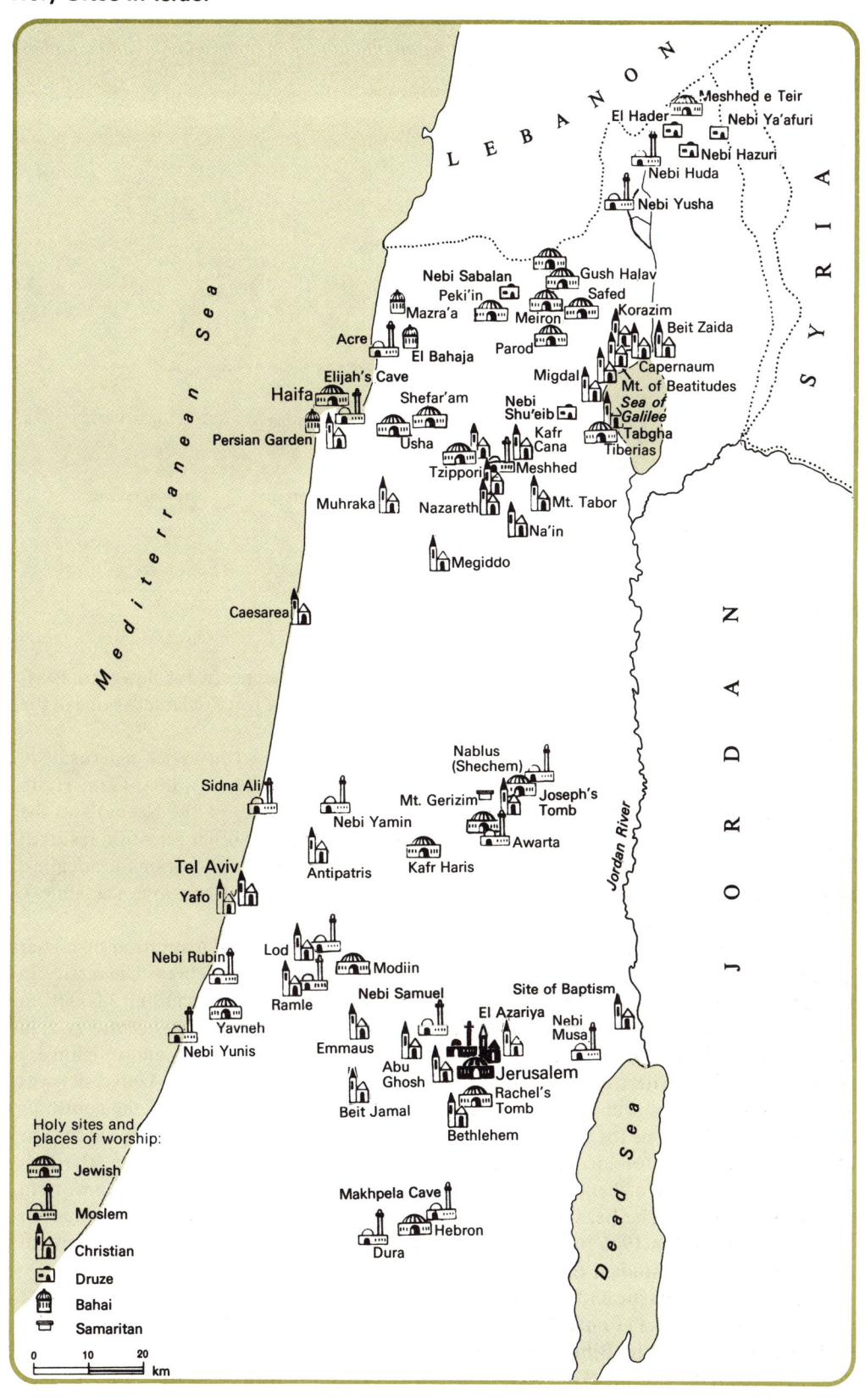

65

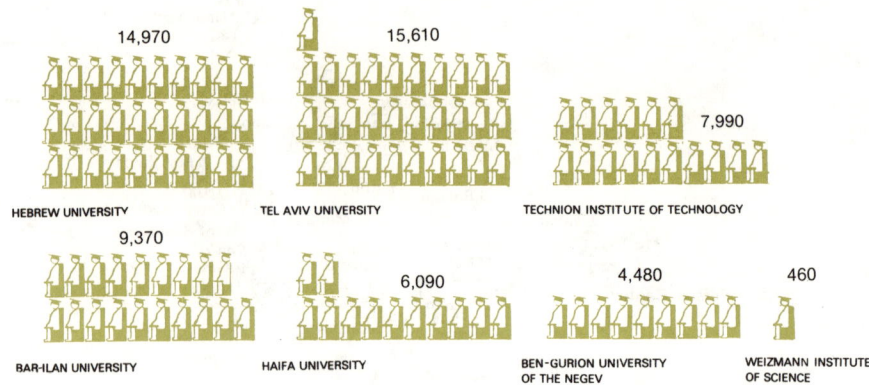

THE SCHOLAR'S ISRAEL

Through the centuries, education has always been a central concern for Jews. In 1981, academically educated persons comprised 15 percent of the work force in Israel — one of the world's highest proportions.

Israel's principal institutions of higher learning are the Hebrew University in Jerusalem, Tel Aviv University, the Technion in Haifa, Bar-Ilan University in Ramat-Gan, Haifa University, Ben-Gurion University (also known as the University of the Negev) and the Weizmann Institute of Science in Rehovot. In addition, there are other scientific research institutes, teachers' training colleges, art schools and music, dance and drama academies. Israel is a leading centre for Jewish studies, and has over 300 *yeshivot* (religious academies), with more than 19,000 students.

The Technion, or Israel Institute of Technology, is Israel's oldest institution of higher learning, founded in 1912; it has today some 8,000 students. The Hebrew University in Jerusalem was opened in 1925; some 15,000 students now study there, including 3,000 from abroad. It has campuses on Mt. Scopus and in West Jerusalem, a medical centre and, in Rehovot, a faculty of agriculture. At Bar-Ilan, Jewish history, philosophy and religion are taught side by side with the humanities and sciences. In 1965, Ben-Gurion University was founded in Beersheba, with the particular aim of opening up the deserts of the south; its departments include one for the study of medicine, and another for arid zones research. The Weizmann Institute, founded in 1934 on the initiative of Chaim Weizmann, the first president of Israel and a chemist by profession, has a world reputation for research work in the natural sciences. The Bezalel Academy is Israel's oldest and most celebrated school of art. It was founded in 1906 by the sculptor Boris Schatz as a national art centre; many of Israel's noted artists studied there.

Among other scholastic and research institutions in Israel today are the Van Leer Institute for the Advancement of Human Culture, the Academy of Sciences, the Shiloah Institute for Middle East Studies, the Biblical Research Institute, the Israel Exploration Society, the Pontifical Institute and the American School of Holy Land Studies.

Higher Education

67

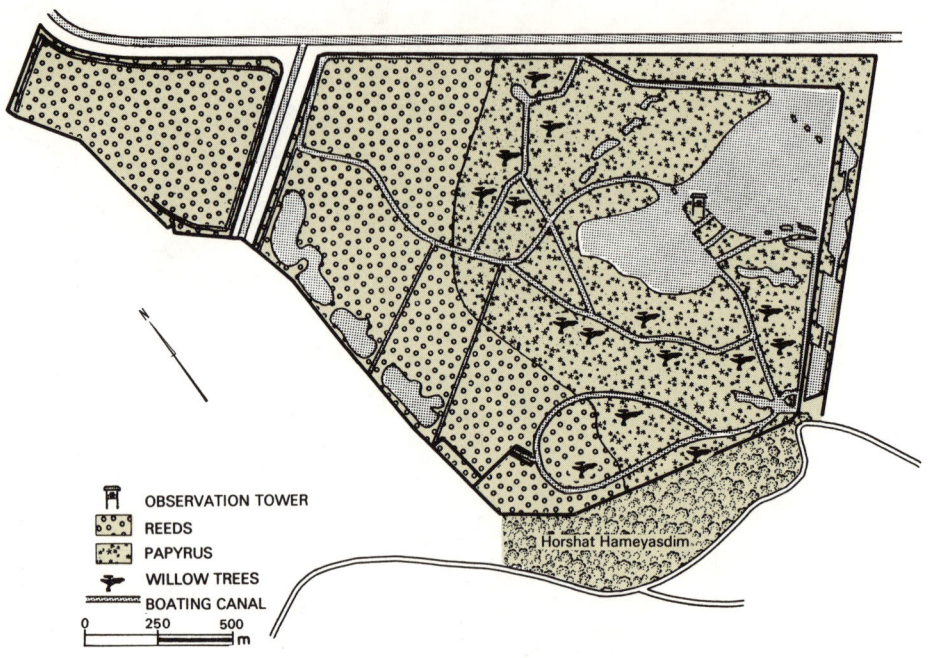

The Hula Nature Reserve

NATURE RESERVES

Israel is a very small country with an extremely varied geological character and landscape. Since the region in which it is situated is a meeting-place of Europe, Asia and Africa, its flora and fauna are not less varied. About 2,500 plants are indigenous to Israel; the animal life is less extensive than it was in biblical times.

From the 7th century — the period of the Moslem conquest — the country began to fall into a state of neglect, reaching its low point during the decline of Turkish rule from the end of the 16th century onwards. Only with modern Jewish resettlement, with its ambitious programme of agricultural development and reafforestation, was its ancient fertility restored.

In recent years, however, Israel, like many other countries, has become increasingly urbanized and industrialized, and the need has been felt to preserve some of the natural scenery in its original condition. Accordingly, in 1963 the Nature Reserves Authority was established to maintain beauty spots throughout the country, guard wild flora and fauna, and make them available for the enjoyment of the public.

There are some 120 nature reserves in Israel, covering about 6 million acres: these are concentrated particularly in the relatively sparsely populated regions of the Galilee and the southern Negev.

National Parks and Nature Reserves

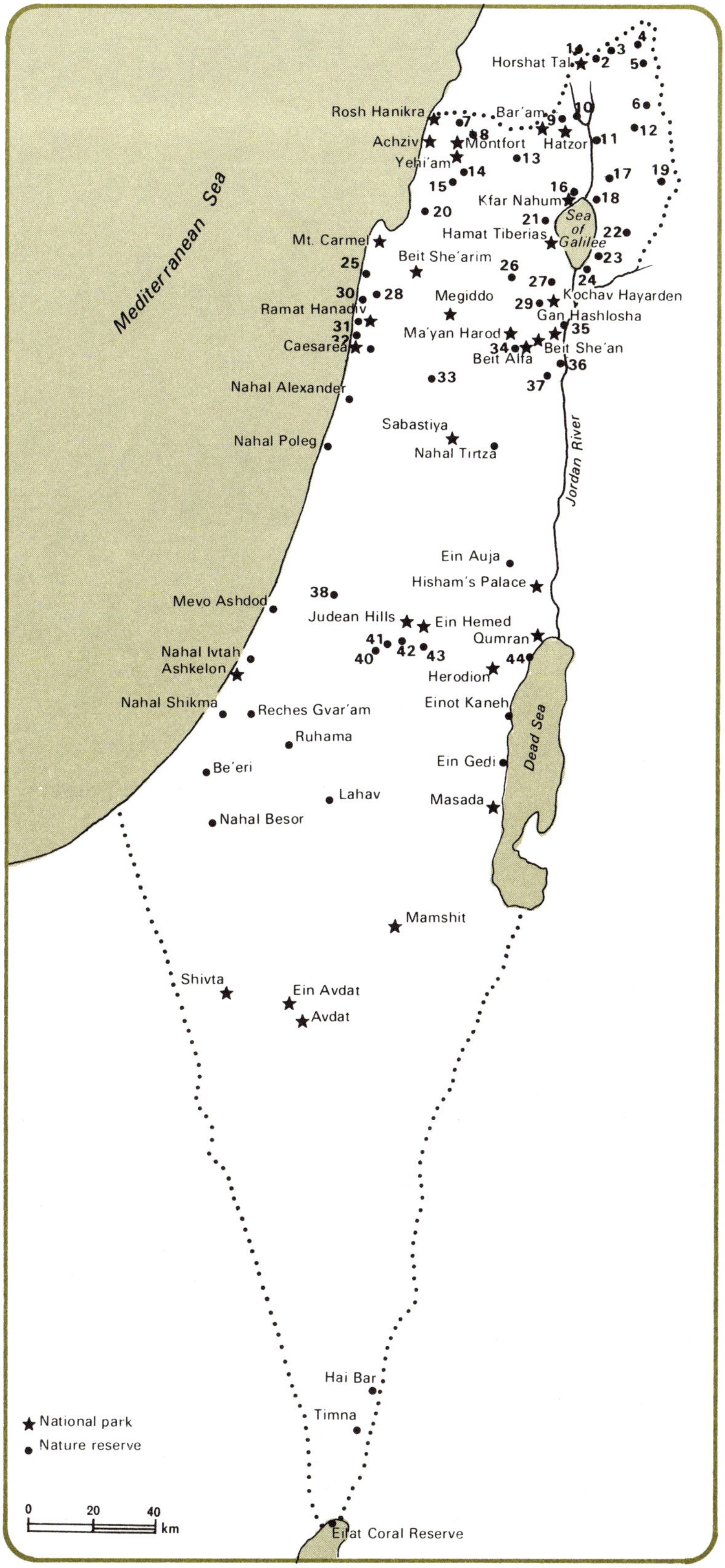

1. Nahal Iyon
2. Nahal Senir
3. Tel Dan
4. Mt. Hermon
5. Ya'ar Odem
6. Mt. Avital
7. Nahal Betzet
8. Nahal Keziv
9. Nahal Dishon
10. Hula
11. Gilbon
12. Mt. Shifon
13. Mt. Meiron
14. Nahal Beit Ha'emek
15. Mt. Gamal
16. Nahal Amud
17. Nahal Zavitan
18. Ya'ar Yahudiya
19. Mt. Peres
20. Tel Afek
21. Arbel
22. Nahal El Al
23. Nahal Meitzar
24. Metzukei On
25. Atlit
26. Mt. Tabor
27. Mitzpeh Eilot
28. Nahal Me'arot
29. Nahal Tav'or
30. Habonim
31. Ya'ar Alona
32. Nahal Taninim
33. Ya'ar Reihan
34. Mt. Gilboa
35. Beit Yosef
36. Ma'oz
37. Tel Saharon
38. Einot Gibeton
39. Wadi Kilt
40. Ma'arat Sorek
41. Nahal Sorek
42. Mt. Hatayasim
43. Hurbat Sa'adim
44. Einot Tzukim

★ National park
● Nature reserve

Playground in Manasseh Forests

YOUTH ACTIVITIES

Israel's youth movements provide more than merely recreation or education. Their members are also conscious of taking an active part in the rebuilding of the country. There are 11 principal organizations, with more than 200,000 members. Most of them are connected with kibbutz movements and/or political parties ranging from right to left. They are: Hano'ar Ha'oved Vehalomed, the Israel Scout Federation, Bnei Akiva (Orthodox), Hashomer Hatzair, Hano'ar Hadati Ha'oved (Orthodox), Hano'ar Ha'oved Hale'umi, Maccabi Hatzair, Dror-Mahanot Ha'olim, Beitar, Ezra (Orthodox), and Hano'ar Hatzioni. Jewish and Arab scouts, nationally federated and affiliated with the International Scout Movement, jointly participate in international jamborees.

Gadna (Youth Corps) is a scout-type organization for boys and girls aged 14-18, run jointly by the Ministry of Education and Culture and the Ministry of Defence. Members participate for one hour a week, and one full day a month. They make an annual trip lasting 4-5 days. Eleventh graders spend 11 days on Gadna's training farms, and twelfth graders devote two weeks a year to National Service — in the form of assistance to outlying villages or in enterprises of educational value.

There are some 30 youth villages throughout Israel run almost entirely by the youngsters themselves, 31 youth hostels, 18 summer camps and 20 field schools.

Youth Facilities

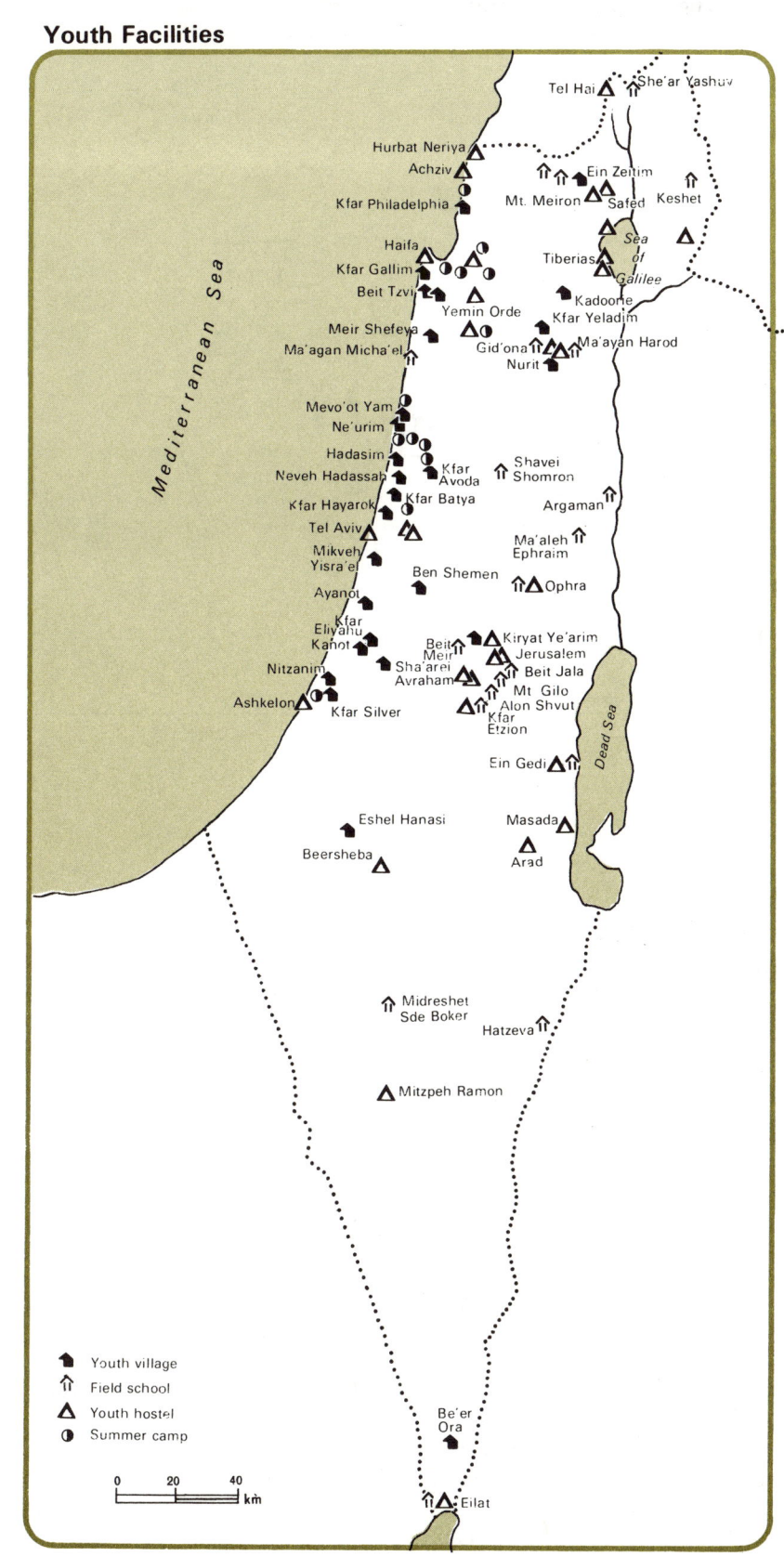

The Wingate Institute

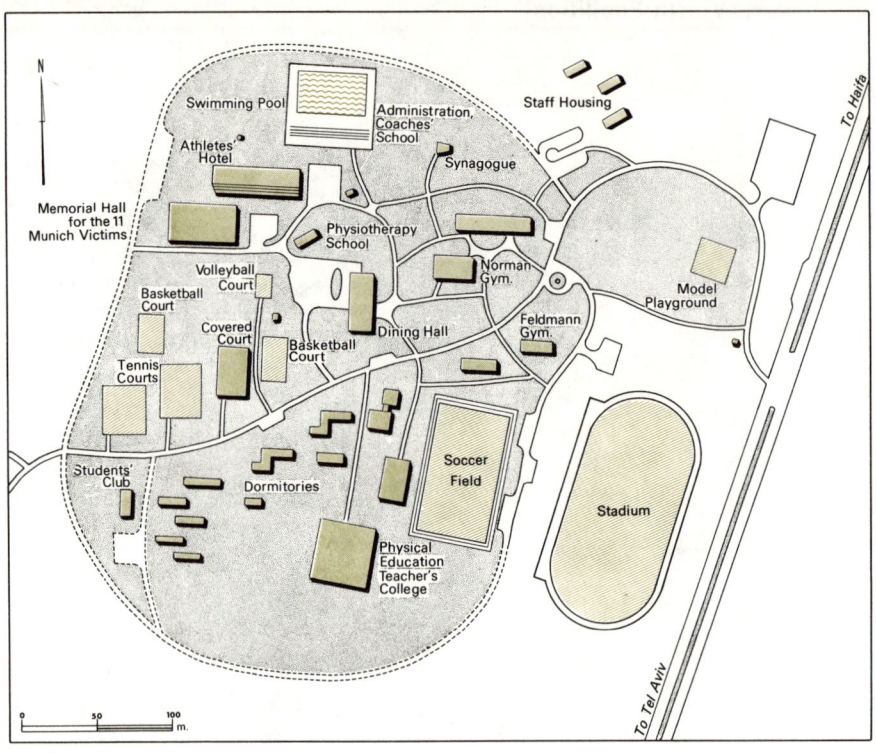

SPORT AND PHYSICAL FITNESS

Israel appreciates the vital role of sport in nation-building as well as in providing recreation. All sports are amateur. Football (soccer), basketball, tennis, swimming, athletics, rowing, sailing, handball, volleyball, gymnastics, weightlifting, wrestling and fencing are amongst the most widespread.

There are five soccer, four basketball and three volleyball leagues — over 1,000 teams in all. There are also high school leagues. The four main sports organizations in Israel are Hapo'el, Maccabi, Elitzur and Beitar.

The Wingate Institute of Physical Education and Sports near Netanya trains sports instructors, coaches and physiotherapists.

Israel regularly takes part in international events such as basketball championships, the Olympic Games, the International Rowing Tournament, the World Soccer Cup, etc. Israel also hosts the Maccabee Games (for Jewish sportsmen, every four years). One of the most popular sports activity is hiking, the main occasion being the annual March to Jerusalem in the tradition of the biblical pilgrimage on Succoth. Tens of thousands of people — including groups from abroad — join in. Other annual community sporting events are the cross-country run around Mt. Tabor, the Hannukah relay race, the 2.8-mile Kinneret swim, and the "Crossing of the Red Sea" in the Gulf of Eilat. Chess is also a popular pastime, and the 1976 Chess Olympiad took place in Israel.

Sports Centres and Activities

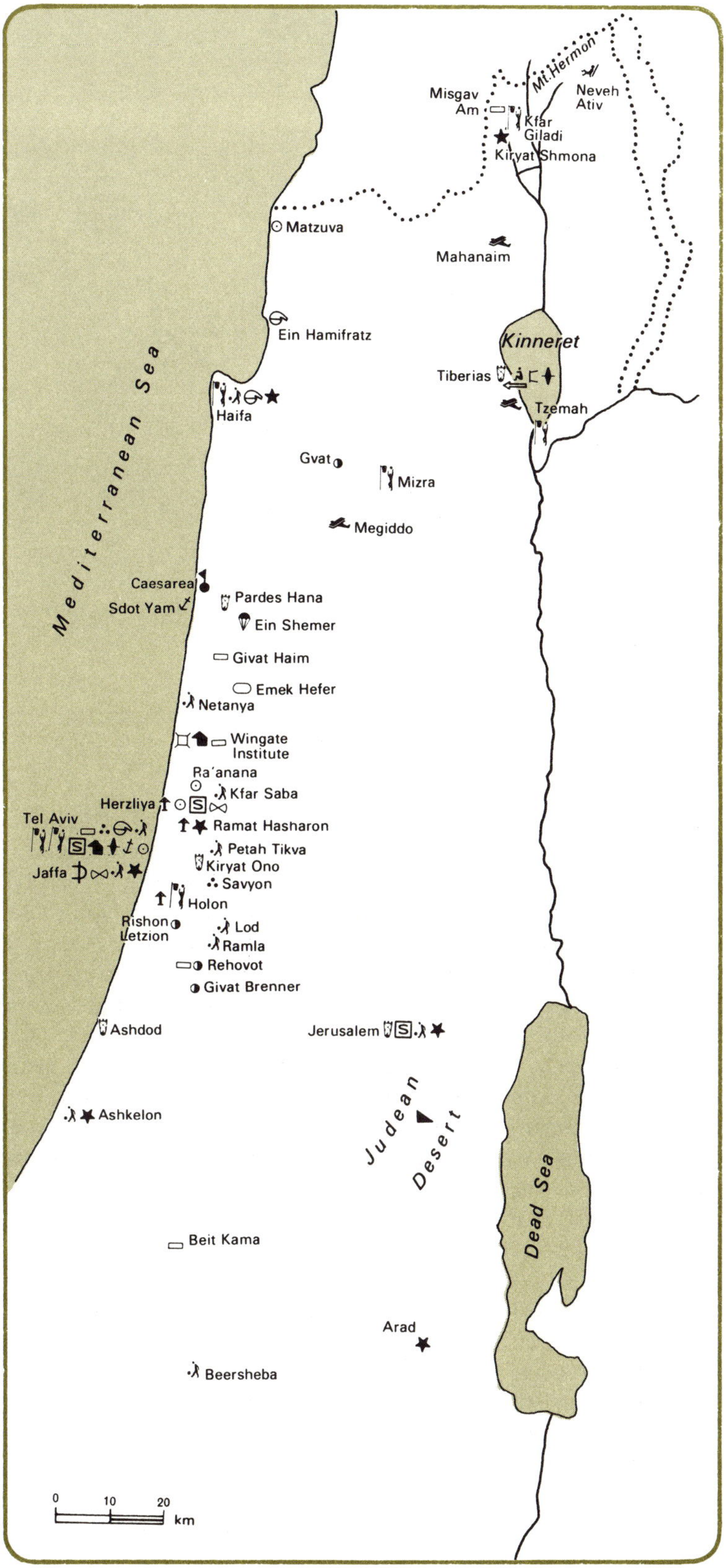

Legend:
- Sports centre
- Football stadium
- Tennis
- Basket-ball
- Olympic swimming pool or centre
- Athletics (Olympic track)
- Gymnastics
- Olympic village
- Country club
- Skiing
- Rowing
- Sailing
- Water-skiing
- Canoeing
- Flying club
- Parachuting
- Gliding
- Shooting range
- Handball
- Mountain climbing
- Squash
- Golf
- Badminton
- Archery
- Bowls

Locations:
Mt. Hermon, Misgav Am, Neveh Ativ, Kfar Giladi, Kiryat Shmona, Matzuva, Mahanaim, Ein Hamifratz, Kinneret, Haifa, Tiberias, Tzemah, Gvat, Mizra, Megiddo, Caesarea, Sdot Yam, Pardes Hana, Ein Shemer, Givat Haim, Emek Hefer, Netanya, Wingate Institute, Ra'anana, Kfar Saba, Herzliya, Ramat Hasharon, Tel Aviv, Petah Tikva, Kiryat Ono, Jaffa, Savyon, Holon, Rishon Letzion, Lod, Ramla, Rehovot, Givat Brenner, Ashdod, Jerusalem, Ashkelon, Beit Kama, Judean Desert, Dead Sea, Arad, Beersheba

Mediterranean Sea

0 10 20 km

The Old City of Jaffa

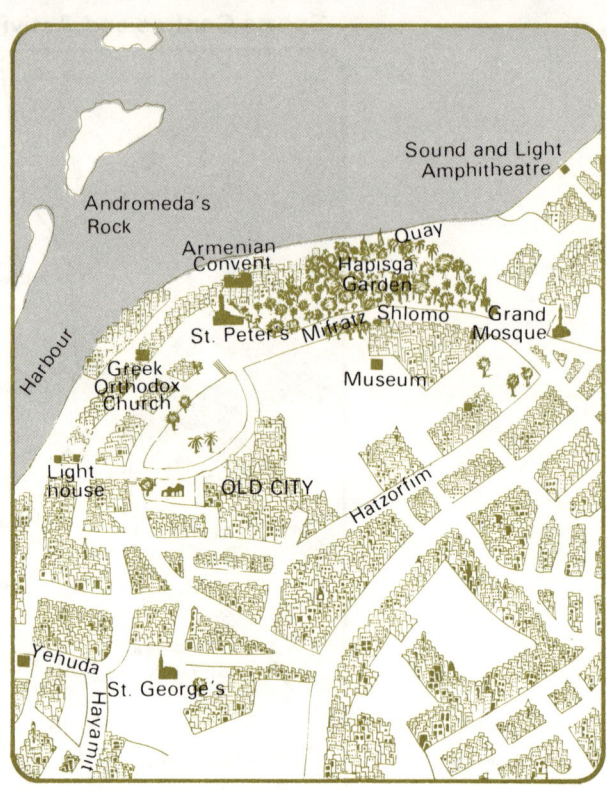

HOLIDAYS AND RELAXATION.

There have always been pilgrims who visit the country to discover its past, to seek out its religious significance and to savour its special atmosphere. Today there are also those who come to see a nation being rebuilt and new modes of living — such as the kibbutz. But there is another aspect of the country, a little unexpected, perhaps, which is becoming known: Israel as a holiday centre, Israel for pleasure and recreation.

Not more than a few hours from any of its main cities, you can enjoy skiing on the slopes of the Hermon, or year-round sunbathing and skin-diving at Eilat on the Red Sea. At the beaches along the Mediterranean one can swim from April to October and, for the more hardy, in winter too. Sailing and water sports are now popular in Israel. The sweet-water Sea of Galilee is a swimming, sailing as well as water-skiing resort.

There are numerous ways of seeing the country. One may travel by internal airline, hire a car or go by bus on one of the guided tours. For the more rugged, there are safari-type tours by command-car in Galilee, the Golan and the Negev.

Those attracted to places with an aura of history, which both evoke images of biblical events and offer sweeping landscapes and views of rolling hills and dales, will not fail to be impressed with Jerusalem which retains the flavour of antiquity despite its modern appendages. Those looking for nightlife, shops and sidewalk cafes, modern luxury hotels by the seaside and a variety of museums and cultural institutions will find all these and more in the lively, sprawling metropolis of Tel Aviv and its satellite towns. For culture-lovers, Tel Aviv and other Israeli cities offer concerts with world-renowned conductors and soloists, ballet, theatre and opera.

Accommodation in Israel is excellent and varied enough for all tastes and pockets, from international luxury hotels to holiday camps and youth hostels for children and students. Some of the best accommodation is to be found in the kibbutz rest-houses around the country.

Holidays and Recreation

- Holiday resort
- Hotel
- Amphitheatre
- Water sports
- Golf
- Skiing
- Museum

0 20 40 km

Index to Map

A
- Abda C6
- Abu Ghosh C5
- Abu Rabi'a, Kseifa C6
- Achziv C2
- Adam D4
- Afek C3
- Afikim D3
- Afula C3
- Afula 'Ilit C3
- Ahihud C2
- Ahuzam B5
- Ai C5
- Ajjul C4
- Akabe C4
- Akko C2
- Akrabe C4
- Allenby Bridge D5
- Alma D2
- Almagor D2
- Alonei Abba C3
- Alonei Habashan D2
- Alumim A6
- Amatzia B5
- Ami'ad D2
- Amirim C2
- Amka C2
- Amman D5
- Anabta C4
- Ani'am D2
- Anin C3
- Arad C6
- Ar'ara C3
- Argaman D4
- Ariel C4
- Arraba C3
- Arraba C3
- Arura C4
- Ashalim B7
- Ashdod B5
- Ashdot Ya'akov D3
- Ashkelon B5
- Atara C4
- Atlit B3
- Avdat B7
- Avihail B4
- Avital C3
- Avnei Eitan D3
- Awarta C4
- Ayanot B5
- Ayelet Hashahar D2
- Azor B4

B
- Bab e-Nakb C4
- Bahan C4
- Baka el-Gharbiya C4
- Banias D2
- Bani Na'im C6
- Bani Suheila A6
- Bar'am C2
- Bardala D4
- Barkai C3
- Barta'a C3
- Bat Shlomo C3
- Bat Yam B4
- Be'eri A6
- Be'er Ora B10
- Beersheba B6
- Be'er Tovia B5
- Beit Alfa C3
- Beit Aula C5
- Beit Dagan B4
- Beit Dajan C4
- Beit E-Rosh B6
- Beit El C5
- Beit Fajjar C5
- Beit Furik C4
- Beit Guvrin B5
- Beit Ha'emek C2
- Beit Hanan B5
- Beit Hananiya B3
- Beit Hanun A5
- Beit Hashita C3
- Beitin C5
- Beit Jala C5
- Beit Jamal B5
- Beit Janin C2
- Beit Kad C3
- Beit Kama B6
- Beit Keshet C3
- Beit Lahiya A5
- Beit Lid C4
- Beit Nehemia B4
- Beit Nur B5
- Beit Oren B3
- Beit Rimon C3
- Beit Sahur C5
- Beit She'an D3
- Beit She'arim C3
- Beit Shemesh B5
- Beitunia C5
- Beit Ur C5
- Beit Yosef D3
- Beit Zur C5
- Beka'ot D4
- Ben Shemen B5
- Besor A6
- Bethlehem C5
- Biddu C5
- Bidya C5
- Binyamina B3
- Bira C5
- Biranit C2
- Birket Ram D2
- Bnei Berak B4
- Bnei Yehuda D3
- Bror Hayil B5
- Budrus B5
- Bu'eina C3
- Burka C4
- Burkin C3
- Bustan Hagalil C2

C
- Caesarea B3
- Capernaum D2
- Carmel C6
- Dabura D2
- Daburiya D3
- Dahiriya B6
- Daliya C3
- Daliyat el-Carmel C3
- Dalton D2
- Dan D2
- Degania D3
- Deir Dibwan C5
- Deir el Balah A6
- Deir el Kilt C5
- Deir el Hajla C5
- Deir Hanna C3
- Deir Nidham C4
- Deir Razih C6
- Devira B6
- Dimona C7
- Dor B3
- Dorot B6
- Dovrat C3
- Dura C6

E
- Eilabun C3
- Eilat B10
- Eilon C2
- Ein Arik C5
- Ein Avdat B7
- Ein Bokek C6
- Ein Carmel B3
- Ein Dor C3
- Ein el Fawar C5
- Ein Fara C4
- Ein Feshha C5
- Ein Gedi C5
- Ein Gev D3
- Ein Hamifratz C2
- Ein Hanatziv D3
- Ein Harod C3
- Ein Hashlosha A6
- Ein Hashofet C3
- Ein Hatzeva C7
- Ein Hemed C5
- Ein Hod B3
- Ein Kuniye D2
- Ein Tamar C7
- Ein Yahav C7
- Ein Zivan D2
- El'azar C5
- El Bira B6
- El Bureij A6
- El Fasayil C4
- Eli Al D3
- Elifelet D2
- Eliyashiv B4
- Elkosh C2
- El Kursi D3
- El Mughazi A6
- El Rom D2
- Erez B5
- Eshel Hanassi B6
- Eshta'ol B5
- Et-Tamad A10
- Even Yehuda B4
- Even Yitzhak C3
- Evron C2
- Eyal B4

F
- Fari'a el Jiftlik D4
- Firasin C3
- Fureidis B3

G
- Ga'aton C2
- Gal-on B5
- Gan Shmuel B3
- Gan Yavneh B5
- Gat B5
- Gaza A6
- Gedera B5
- Geia B5
- Gesher D3
- Geshur D3
- Gevulot A6
- Gid'ona C3
- Gilat B6
- Gilgal C4
- Ginegar C3
- Ginossar D3
- Gitit C4
- Giv'at Ada C5
- Giv'atayim B4
- Giv'at Brenner B5
- Giv'at Haim B4
- Giv'at Koah B4
- Giv'at Olga B3
- Giv'at Oz C3
- Giv'at Yo'av D3
- Gonen D2
- Goren C2
- Grofit C9
- Gvar Am B5

H
- Habonim C3
- Hadera B3
- Hahotrim B3
- Haifa B3
- Halhul C5
- Hama'apil B4
- Hamadiya D3
- Hamei Zohar C6
- Hamra C4
- Hanita C2
- Hao'gen B4
- Ha'on D3
- Haras C5
- Haris C4
- Hasolelim C3
- Hatzerim B6
- Hatzeva "Ir Ovot" C7
- Hatzeva (Moshav) C7
- Hatzor B7
- Hayogev C3
- Hazon C3
- Hazore'a C3
- Hazor'im D3
- Hebron C5
- Herzliya B4
- Hizma C5
- Hod Hasharon B4
- Holon B4
- Horshim B4
- Hukok D2
- Hulata D2
- Hulda B5
- Hushniyeh D2
- Huwara C4

I
- I'dan C7
- Idna B5
- Ilaniya C3
- Immatin C4
- Issfiya C3

J
- Jaba C4
- Jaba C5
- Jalkamus C3
- Jalud C4
- Janiya C5
- Jarba C4
- Jatt C2
- Jenin C3
- Jericho C5
- Jerusalem C5
- Jifna C5
- Judeida C2

K
- Kabalan C4
- Kabatiye C4
- Kabri C2
- Kafr Cana C3
- Kafr Dan C3
- Kafr Ein C4
- Kafr el Labad C4
- Kafr Kaddum C4
- Kafr Kama C3
- Kafr Kassem B4
- Kafr Lakif C4
- Kafr Malik C4
- Kafr Sumei C2
- Kafr Thult C4
- Kalansuwa B4
- Kalkilya B4
- Kalya C5
- Karmiel C2
- Karmiya A5
- Karnei Shomron C4
- Kasr el Yahud D5
- Katif A6
- Katrin D2
- Kedumim C4
- Keren Maharal B3
- Kerem Shalom A6
- Keshet D2
- Ketziot A7
- Kfar Ahim B5
- Kfar Aza A6
- Kfar Azar B4
- Kfar Blum D2
- Kfar Darom A6
- Kfar Etziyon C5
- Kfar Gil'adi D2
- Kfar Habad B4
- Kfar Hahoresh C3
- Kfar Haro'eh B4
- Kfar Hassidim C3
- Kfar Masaryk C2
- Kfar Mordechai B5
- Kfar Rosh Hanikra C2
- Kfar Ruppin D3
- Kfar Saba B4
- Kfar Shamai C2
- Kfar Shmaryahu B4
- Kfar Shmuel B5
- Kfar Szold C2
- Kfar Tapuah C4
- Kfar Tavor C3
- Kfar Vitkin B4
- Kfar Warburg B5
- Kfar Yehezkel C3
- Kfar Yona B4
- Kfar Zechariya B5
- Kfar Zeitim C3
- Khaspin D3
- Khan Yunis A6
- Kharbata C5
- Khirbet el Auja el Fawka C4
- Kh. el Mafjar D5
- Khirbet el Malikh C4
- Kh. Kumran C5
- Kibya C4
- Kinneret D3
- Kiryat Anavim C5
- Kiryat Arba C5
- Kiryat Ata C3
- Kiryat Bialik C3
- Kiryat Gat B5
- Kiryat Haim C3
- Kiryat Malachi B5
- Kiryat Motzkin C3
- Kiryat Ono B4
- Kiryat Shmona D2
- Kiryat Tiv'on C3
- Kiryat Yam C3
- Kisufim A6
- Kochav Hashahar C5
- Korazim D2
- Ktura C9
- Kufeirat C3
- Kuneitra D2

L
- Lachish B5
- Lahav B6
- Lahavot Habashan D2
- Lahavot Haviva C4
- Lapidot C2
- Lasifar C6
- Latrun B5
- Lavi C3
- Liman C2
- Lod B5
- Lod Airport B4
- Lohamei Hageta'ot C2
- Lubban Sharkiya C4
- Luzit B5

M
- Ma'abarot B4
- Ma'agan D3
- Ma'agan Michael B3
- Ma'aleh Adummim C5
- Ma'aleh Efraim C4
- Ma'aleh Gamla D2
- Ma'aleh Hahamisha C5
- Ma'alot C3
- Ma'an D8
- Ma'anit C3
- Magen A6
- Maghar C2
- Mahanayim D2
- Majdal Shams D2
- Majd el-Krum C2
- Mamshit C7
- Mansura D2
- Ma'on C6
- Ma'oz Haim D3
- Marda C5
- Mar Saba C5
- Mas'ada D2
- Mash'abei Sadeh B7
- Mash'en B5
- Massu'a D4
- Mata C5
- Matzliah B5
- Matzuva C2
- Mavki'im B5
- Mazkeret Batiya B5
- Mazra'a C4
- Mechora C4
- Mefalsim B6
- Megadim B3
- Megiddo C3
- Mehola D4
- Mei Ami C3
- Meiron C2
- Menara D2
- Merhaviya C3
- Merkaz Alon Shevut C5
- Merkaz Sapir C8
- Merom Golan D2
- Mesilat Tzion C5
- Metulla D2
- Metzada C6
- Metzad Bokek C6
- Mevo Beitar C5
- Mevo Hamma D3
- Mevo Horon C5
- Mevo Modi'im B5
- Michmoret B4
- Migdal Ha'emek C3
- Misgav Am D2
- Mishmar Ayalon B5
- Mishmar Ha'emek C3
- Mishmar Hanegev B6
- Mishmeret B4
- Mishor Adummim C5
- Misilya C4
- Mitzpa D3
- Mitzpeh Ramon B8
- Mitzpeh Shalem C5
- Mivtahim A6
- Mizra C3
- Monfort C2
- Morag A6
- Moran C2
- Motza B5
- Mt. Herodion C5
- Mt. of Beatitudes D2
- Musmus C3

N
- Na'an B5
- Nablus C4
- Nahala B5
- Nahalal C3
- Nahal Malkishu'a C3
- Nahal Oz A6
- Nahariya C2
- Nahsholim B3
- Nazareth C3
- Nazlat C4
- Nebi Musa C5
- Nebi Shueib C3
- Negba B5
- Nehora B5
- Nehusha B5
- Ne'ot Golan D3
- Ne'ot Hakikar C7
- Ne'ot Mordechai D2
- Nesher C3
- Ness Harim C5
- Ness Tziona B5
- Netanya B4
- Netiv Halamed Hey b5
- Netivot B6
- Netzarim A6
- Netzer Hazani A6
- Nevatim B6
- Neveh Ativ D2
- Neveh Eitan D3
- Neveh Ur D3
- Neveh Ya'akov C5
- Neveh Yam B3
- Neveh Zohar C6
- Nir Am B6
- Nir Banim B5
- Nir David C3
- Nir Galim B5
- Nirim A6
- Nir Oz A6
- Nir Yaffe C3
- Nir Yitzhak A6
- Nitzana A7
- Nitzanei Oz B4
- Nitzanim B5
- No'am B5
- Nordiya B4
- Nov D3
- Nurit C3
- Nuseirat A6

O
- Odem D2
- Ofakim B6
- Ofra C5
- Omer B6
- Ora C5
- Or Haner B5
- Oron B7
- Or Tal D2
- Or Yehuda B4

P
- Palmahim B5
- Paran C8
- Pardess Hanna-Karkur Parod C2 B3
- Patish B6
- Pedaya B5
- Peduyim B6
- Peki'in C2
- Perazon C3
- Petah Tikva B4
- Petzael C4
- Poriya D3
- Pri Gan A6

R
- Ra'anana B4
- Raba C4
- Rabud C6
- Rafa A6
- Rahat B6
- Rama C4
- Rama C2
- Ramallah C5
- Ramat Gan B4
- Ramat Hadar B4
- Ramat Hakovesh B4
- Ramat Hasharon B4
- Ramat Hashofet C3
- Ramat Magshimim D3
- Ramat Rachel C5
- Ramat Raziel C5
- Ramat Yohanan C3
- Ramla B5
- Rammun C5
- Ram On C3
- Ramot D3
- Ramot Hashavim B4
- Ramot Naftali D2
- Ramta D2
- Ramthaniyeh D2
- Rannen B6
- Rantis C4
- Regavim C3
- Rehov D3
- Rehovot B5
- Re'im A6
- Reshafim D3
- Retamim B7
- Revadim B5
- Revaya C3
- Revivim B7
- Rishon Letzion B5
- Roglit B5
- Rosh Ha'ayin B4
- Rosh Pina D2
- Rosh Tzurim C5
- Ruhama B6
- Rumana C3

S
- Sa'ad A6
- Sa'ar C2
- Sabastiya C4
- Safad D2
- Sakhnin C2
- Salem C4
- Salfit C4
- Samar B9
- Samua C5
- Sanur C4
- Sarid C3
- Sasa C2
- Satriye D4
- Sde Boker B7
- Sde Eliahu D3
- Sde Ilan C3
- Sde Moshe B5
- Sde Nahum D3
- Sde Yitzhak B4
- Sederot B6
- Segev C3
- Sha'al D2
- Sha'alavim B5
- Shabtin C5
- Shafir B5
- Shamir D2
- Shavei Tzion C2
- Shefayim B4
- Shetula C2
- Shfar'am C3
- Shibbolim B6
- Shilo C4
- Shivta B7
- Shlomtzion C4
- Shomera C2
- Shomron C4
- Shoval B6
- Shuweika C4
- Shuyukh C5
- Sifsufa C2
- Silat el Haratiya C3
- Sinjil C4
- Sir C4
- Siris C4
- Snir D2
- Sodom C7
- Sufa A6
- Surif C5
- Susita D3

T
- Tabgha D3
- Taiyba B4
- Taiyba C5
- Talluza C4
- Talmei Bilu B6
- Talmei Eliezer B3
- Talmei Yosef A6
- Tal Shahar B5
- Tamra C3
- Tamun C4
- Tarkumiya C5
- Tayasir C4
- Te'ashur B6
- Tel Adashim C3
- Telalim B7
- Tel Arad C6
- Tel Aviv—Yafo B4
- Tel Hashomer B4
- Tel Jericho C5
- Tel Mond B4
- Tiberias D3
- Timmorim B5
- Timna B9
- Tira B4
- Tira C5
- Tirat Carmel B3
- Tirat Tzevi D4
- Tirosh B5
- Tubas C4
- Tulkarm C4
- Tur'an C3
- Turmus Aiya C4
- Tuval C2
- Tushiya A6
- Tyre C2
- Tze'elim A6
- Tzippori C3
- Tzofar C8
- Tzuriel C2
- Tzur Natan C4

U
- Um el Fahm C3
- Urim A6

W
- Wadi Fukin C5

Y
- Ya'ad C3
- Ya'bad C5
- Yachini B6
- Yad Mordechai B5
- Yagur C3
- Yahel C9
- Yakum B4
- Yardena D3
- Yasid C4
- Yatir B6
- Yatta C6
- Yavne'el D3
- Yavneh B5
- Yedidya B4
- Yehiam C2
- Yehud B4
- Yehudiya D2
- Yeroham B7
- Yesh'a A6
- Yir'on C2
- Yitav C5
- Yizre'el C3
- Yodfat C3
- Yokne'am C3
- Yonatan D2
- Yotvata C9

Z
- Zar'it C2
- Zibda C3
- Zichron Ya'akov B3
- Zikim A5
- Zohar B5

MAP OF ISRAEL

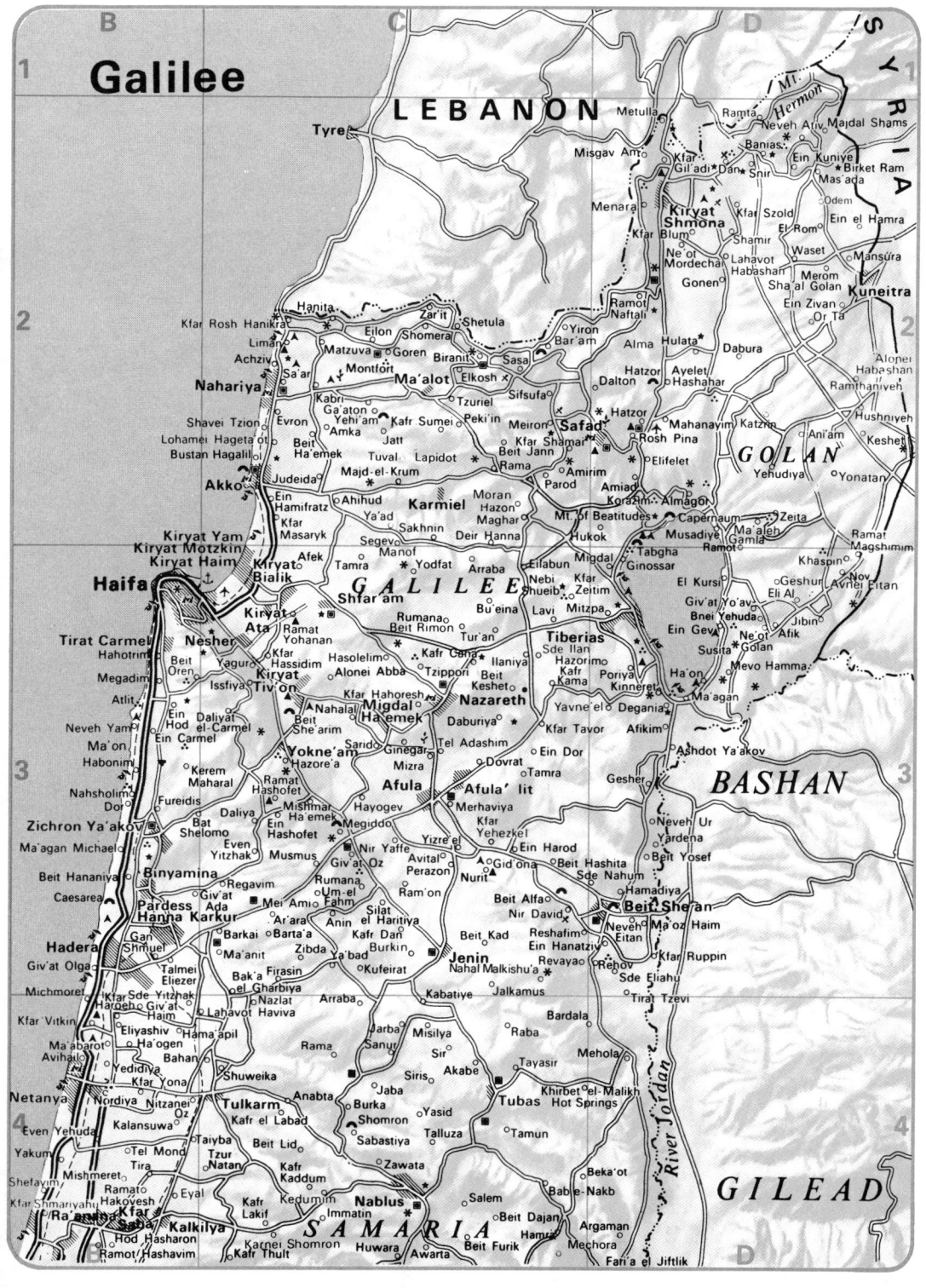

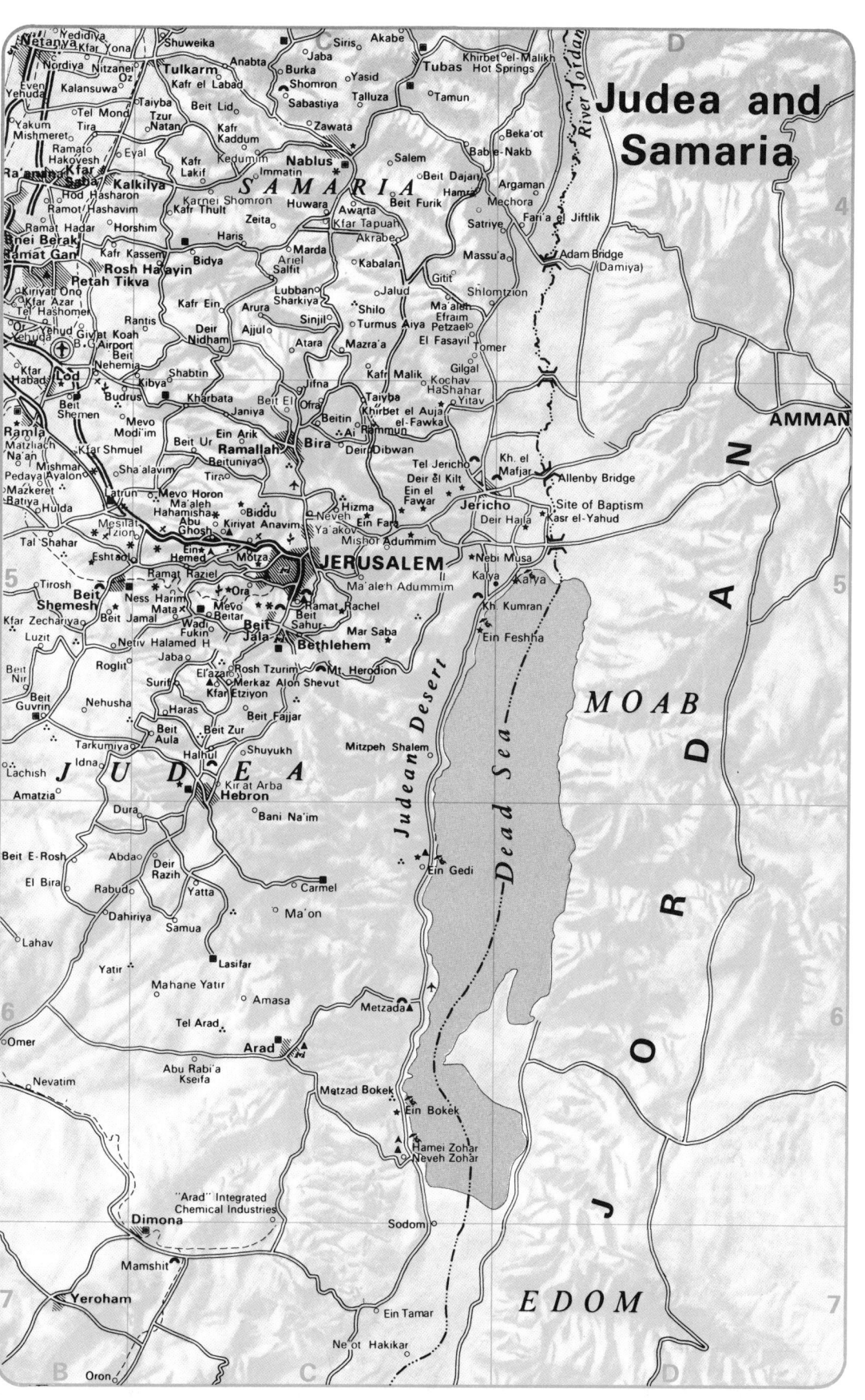

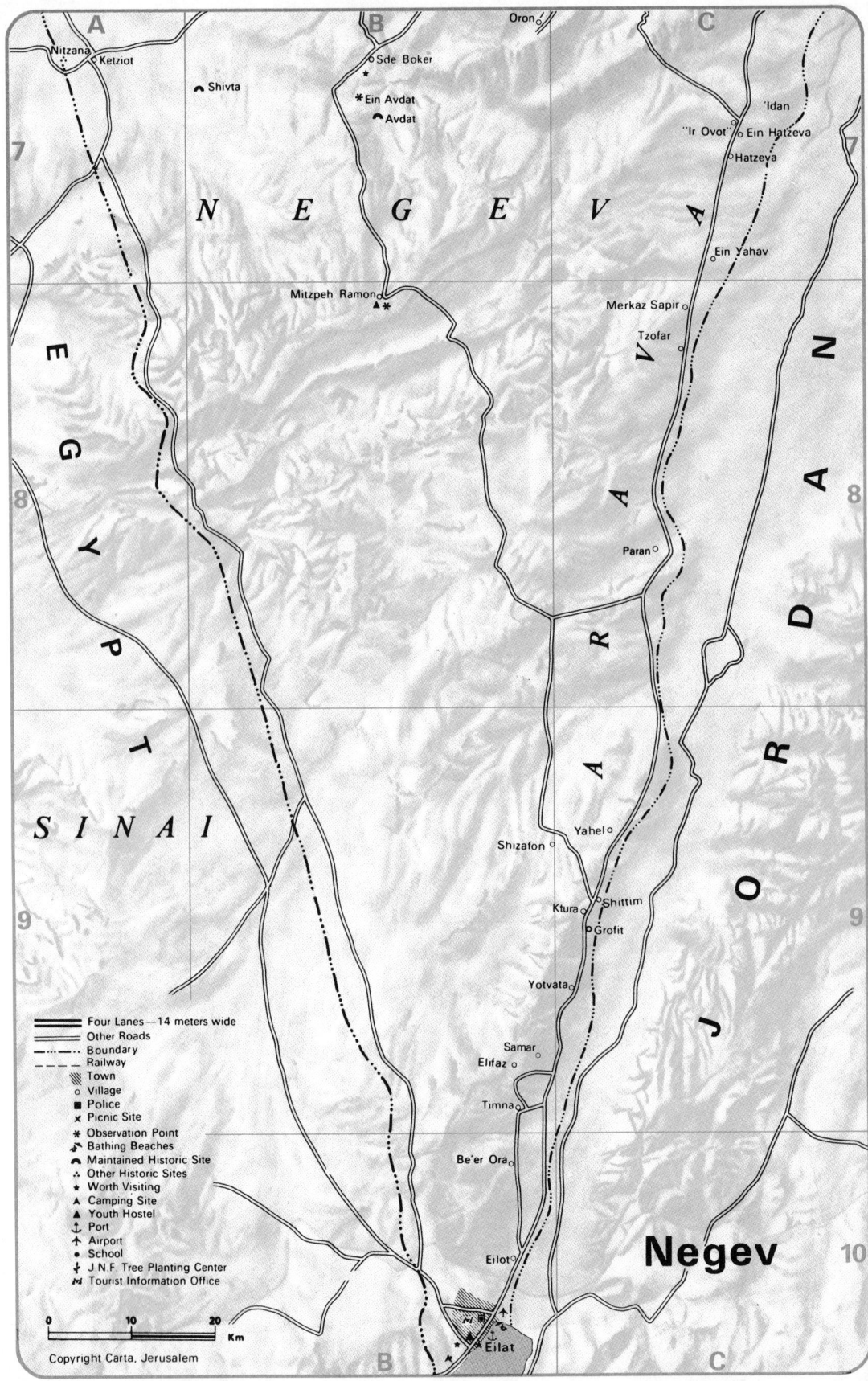